Irish Fairy Tales

EDMUND LEAMY

Mercier Press
PO Box 5, 5 French Church Street, Cork
24 Lower Abbey Street, Dublin 1

First published 1906
This edition © Mercier Press, 1978

A CIP record for this book is available from the British Library.

ISBN 0 85342 917 0

14 13 12 11 10 9 8 7 6 5 4

Printed in Ireland by Colour Books Ltd.

CONTENTS

PRINCESS FINOLA AND THE DWARF

A long, long time ago there lived in a little hut in the midst of a bare, brown, lonely moor an old woman and a young girl. The old woman was withered, sour-tempered, and dumb. The young girl was as sweet and as fresh as an opening rosebud, and her voice was as musical as the whisper of a stream in the woods in the hot days of summer. The little hut, made of branches woven closely together, was shaped like a beehive. In the centre of the hut a fire burned night and day from year's end to year's end, though it was never touched or tended by human hand. In the cold days and nights of winter it gave out light and heat that made the hut cosy and warm, but in the summer nights and days it gave out light only. With their heads to the wall of the hut and their feet towards the fire were two sleeping-couches—one of plain woodwork, in which slept the old woman; the other was Finola's. It was of bog-oak, polished as a looking-glass, and on it were carved flowers and birds of all kinds, that gleamed and shone in the light of the fire. This couch was fit for a princess, and a princess Finola was, though she did not know it herself.

Outside the hut the bare, brown, lonely moor stretched for miles on every side, but towards the east it was bounded by a range of mountains that looked to Finola blue in the daytime, but which put on a hundred changing colours as the sun went down. Nowhere was a house to be seen, nor a tree, nor a flower, nor sign of any living thing. From morning till night, nor hum of bee, nor song of bird, nor voice of man, nor any sound fell on Finola's ears. When the storm was in the air the great waves thundered on the shore beyond the mountains, and the wind shouted in the glens; but when it sped across the moor it lost its voice, and passed as silently as the dead. At first the silence frightened Finola, but she got used to it after a time, and often broke it by talking to herself and singing.

The only other person beside the old woman Finola ever saw was a dumb dwarf who, mounted on a broken-down horse, came once a month to the hut, bringing with him a sack of corn for the old woman and Finola. Although he couldn't speak to her, Finola was always glad to see the dwarf and his old horse, and she used to give them cake made with her own white hands. As for the dwarf he would have died for the little princess, he was so much in love with her, and often and often his heart was heavy and sad as he thought of her pining away in the lonely moor.

It chanced that he came one day, and she did not, as usual, come out to greet him. He made signs to the old woman, but she took up a stick and struck him, and beat his horse and drove him away; but as he was leaving he caught a glimpse of Finola at the door of the hut, and saw that she was crying. This sight made him so very miserable that he could think of nothing else but her sad face that he had always seen so bright, and he allowed the old horse to go on without minding where he was going. Suddenly he heard a voice saying: 'It is time for you to come.'

6

The dwarf looked, and right before him, at the foot of a green hill, was a little man not half as big as himself, dressed in a green jacket with brass bottons, and a red cap and tassel.

'It is time for you to come,' he said the second time; 'but you are welcome, anyhow. Get off your horse and come in with me, that I may touch your lips with the want of speech, that we may have a talk together.

The dwarf got off his horse and followed the little man through a hole in the side of a green hill. The hole was so small that he had to go on his hands and knees to pass through it, and when he was able to stand he was only the same height as the little fairyman. After walking three or four steps they were in a splendid room, as bright as day. Diamonds sparkled in the roof as stars sparkle in the sky when the night is without a cloud. The roof rested on golden pillars, and between the pillars were silver lamps, but their light was dimmed by that of the diamonds. In the middle of the room was a table, on which were two golden plates and two silver knives and forks, and a brass bell as big as a hazelnut, and beside the table were two little chairs covered with blue silk and satin.

'Take a chair,' said the fairy, 'and I will ring for the wand of speech.'

The dwarf sat down, and the fairyman rang the little brass bell, and in came a little weeny dwarf no bigger than your hand.

'Bring me the wand of speech,' said the fairy, and the weeny dwarf bowed three times and walked out backwards, and in a minute he returned, carrying a little black wand with a red berry at the top of it, and, giving it to the fairy, he bowed three times and walked out backwards as he had done before.

The little man waved the rod three times over the dwarf, and struck him once on the right shoulder and once on the left shoulder, and then touched his lips with the red berry, and said: 'Speak!'

The dwarf spoke, and he was so rejoiced at hearing the sound of his own voice that he danced about the room.

'Who are you at all, at all?' said he to the fairy.

'Who is yourself?' said the fairy. 'But come before we have any talk let us have something to eat, for I am sure you are hungry.'

Then they sat down to table, and the fairy rang the little brass bell twice, and the weeny dwarf brought in two boiled snails in their shells, and when they had eaten the snails he brought in a dormouse, and when they had eaten the dormouse he brought in two wrens, and when they had eaten the wrens he brought in two nuts full of wine, and they became very merry, and the fairyman sang *Cooleen dhas*, and the dwarf sang *The little blackbird of the glen*.

'Did you ever hear the *Foggy Dew*?' said the fairy.

'No,' said the dwarf.

'Well, then, I'll give it to you; but we must have some more wine.'

And the wine was brought, and he sang the *Foggy Dew*, and the dwarf said it was the sweetest song he had ever heard, and that the fairyman's voice would coax the birds off the bushes.

'You asked me who I am?' said the fairy.

'I did,' said the dwarf.

'And I asked you who is yourself?'

'You did,' said the dwarf.

'And who are you, then?'

'Well, to tell the truth, I don't know,' said the dwarf, and he blushed like a rose.

'Well, tell me what you know about yourself.'

'I remember nothing at all,' said the dwarf, 'before the day I found myself going along with a crowd of all sorts of people to the great fair of the Liffey. We had to pass by the king's palace on our way, and as we were passing the king sent for a band of jugglers to come and show their tricks before him. I followed the jugglers to look on, and when the play was over the king called me to him, and asked me who I was and where I came from. I was dumb then, and couldn't answer; but even if I could speak I could not tell him what he wanted to know, for I remember nothing of myself before that day. Then the king asked the jugglers, but they knew nothing about me, and no one knew anything, and then the king said he would take me into his service; and the only work I have to do is to go once a month with a bag of corn to the hut on the lonely moor.'

'And there you fell in love with the little princess,' said the fairy, winking at the dwarf.

The poor dwarf blushed twice as much as he had done before.

'You need not blush,' said the fairy; 'it is a good man's case. And now tell me, truly, do you love the princess, and what would you give to free her from the spell of the enchantment that is over her?'

'I would give my life,' said the dwarf.

'Well, then, listen to me,' said the fairy. 'The Princess Finola was banished to the lonely moor by the king, your master. He killed her father, who

was the rightful king, and would have killed Finola,
only he was told by an old sorceress that if he
killed her he would die himself on the same day,
and she advised him to banish her to the lonely
moor, and she said she would fling a spell of
enchantment over it, and that until the spell was
broken Finola could not leave the moor. And the
sorceress also promised that she would send an old
woman to watch over the princess by night and by
day, so that no harm should come to her; but she
told the king that he himself should select a
messenger to take food to the hut, and that he
should look out for some one who had never seen
or heard of the princess, and whom he could trust
never to tell anyone anything about her; and that is
the reason he selected you.'

'Since you know so much,' said the dwarf, 'can
you tell me who I am, and where I came from?'

'You will know that time enough,' said the fairy.
'I have given you back your speech. It will depend
solely on yourself whether you will get back your
memory of who and what you were before the day
you entered the king's service. But are you really
willing to try and break the spell of enchantment
and free the princess?'

'I am,' said the dwarf.

'Whatever it will cost you?'

'Yes, if it cost me my life,' said the dwarf; 'but
tell me, how can the spell be broken?'

'Oh, it is easy enough to break the spell if you
have the weapons,' said the fairy.

'And what are they, and where are they?' said
the dwarf.

'The spear of the shining haft and the dark blue
blade and the silver shield,' said the fairy. 'They are

on the farther bank of the Mystic Lake in the Island of the Western Seas. They are there for the man who is bold enough to seek them. If you are the man who will bring them back to the lonely moor you will only have to strike the shield three times with the haft, and three times with the blade of the spear, and the silence of the moor will be broken for ever, the spell of enchantment will be removed, and the princess will be free.'

'I will set out at once,' said the dwarf jumping from his chair.

'And whatever it cost you,' said the fairy, 'will you pay the price?'

'I will,' said the dwarf.

'Well, then, mount your horse, give him his head, and he will take you to the shore opposite the Island of the Mystic Lake. You must cross to the island on his back, and make your way through the water-steeds that swim around the island night and day to guard it; but woe betide you if you attempt to cross without paying the price, for if you do the angry water-steeds will rend you and your horse to pieces. And when you come to the Mystic Lake you must wait until the waters are as red as wine, and then swim your horse across it, and on the farther side you will find the spear and shield; but woe betide you if you attempt to cross the lake before you pay the price, for if you do, the black Cormorants of the Western Seas will pick the flesh from your bones.'

'What is the price?' said the dwarf.

'You will know that time enough,' said the fairy; 'but now go, and good luck go with you.'

The dwarf thanked the fairy, and said good-bye! He then threw the reins on his horse's neck, and started up the hill, that seemed to grow bigger and bigger as he ascended, and the dwarf soon found that what he took for a hill was a great mountain. After travelling all the day, toiling up by steep crags and heathery passes, he reached the top as the sun was setting in the ocean, and he saw far below him out in the waters the Island of the Mystic Lake.

He began his descent to the shore, but long before he reached it the sun had set, and darkness, unpierced by a single star, dropped upon the sea. The old horse, worn out by his long and painful journey, sank beneath him, and the dwarf was so tired that he rolled off his back and fell asleep by his side.

He awoke at the breaking of the morning, and saw that he was almost at the water's edge. He looked out to sea, and saw the island, but nowhere could he see the water-steeds, and he began to fear he must have taken a wrong course in the night, and that the island before him was not the one he was in search of. But even while he was so thinking he heard fierce and angry snortings, and, coming swiftly from the island to the shore, he saw the swimming and prancing steeds. Sometimes their heads and manes only were visible, and sometimes, rearing, they rose half out of the water, and, striking it with their hoofs, churned it into foam, and tossed the white spray to the skies. As they approached nearer and nearer their snortings became more terrible, and their nostrils shot forth clouds of vapour. The dwarf trembled at the sight and sound, and his old horse, quivering in every limb, moaned piteously, as if in pain. On came the steeds, until they almost touched the shore, then rearing, they seemed about to spring on to it. The frightened dwarf turned his head to fly, and as he did so he heard the twang of a golden harp, and right before him who should he see but the little man of the hills, holding a harp in one hand and striking the strings with the other.

'Are you ready to pay the price?' said he, nodding gaily to the dwarf.

As he asked the question, the listening water-steeds snorted more furiously than ever.

'Are you ready to pay the price?' said the little man a second time.

A shower of spray, tossed on shore by the angry steeds, drenched the dwarf to the skin, and sent a cold shiver to his bones, and he was so terrified that he could not answer.

'For the third and last time, are you ready to pay the price?' asked the fairy, as he flung the harp behind him and turned to depart.

When the dwarf saw him going he thought of the little princess in the lonely moor, and his courage came back, and he answered bravely:

'Yes, I am ready.'

The water-steeds, hearing his answer, and snorting with rage, struck the shore with their pounding hoofs.

'Back to your waves!' cried the little harper; and as he ran his fingers across his lyre, the frightened steeds drew back into the waters.

'What is the price?' asked the dwarf.

'Your right eye,' said the fairy; and before the dwarf could say a word, the fairy scooped out the eye with his finger, and put it into his pocket.

The dwarf suffered most terrible agony; but he resolved to bear it for the sake of the little princess.

Then the fairy sat down on a rock at the edge of the sea, and, after striking a few notes, he began to play the *Strains of Slumber*.

The sound crept along the waters, and the steeds, so ferocious a moment before, became perfectly still. They had no longer any motion of their own, and they floated on the top of the tide like foam before a breeze.

'Now,' said the fairy, as he led the dwarf's horse to the edge of the tide.

The dwarf urged the horse into the water, and once out of his depth, the old horse struck out boldly for the island. The sleeping water-steeds drifted helplessly against him, and in a short time he reached the island safely, and he neighed joyously as his hoofs touched solid ground.

The dwarf rode on and on, until he came to a bridle-path, and following this, it led him up through winding lanes, bordered with golden furze that filled the air with fragrance, and brought him to the summit of the green hills that girdled and looked down on the Mystic Lake. Here the horse stopped of his own accord, and the dwarf's heart beat quickly as his eye rested on the lake, that, clipped round by the ring of hills, seemed in the breezeless and sunlit air—

> As still as death,
> And as bright as life can be.

After gazing at it for a long time, he dismounted, and lay at his ease in the pleasant grass. Hour after hour passed, but no change came over the face of the waters, and when the night fell sleep closed the eyelids of the dwarf.

The song of the lark awoke him in the early

morning, and, starting up, he looked at the lake, but its waters were as bright as they had been the day before.

Towards midday he beheld what he thought was a black cloud sailing across the sky from east to west. It seemed to grow larger as it came nearer and nearer, and when it was high above the lake he saw it was a huge bird, the shadow of whose outstretched wings darkened the waters of the lake; and the dwarf knew it was one of the Cormorants of the Western Seas. As it descended slowly, he saw that it held in one of its claws a branch of a tree larger than a full-grown oak, and laden with clusters of ripe red berries. It alighted at some distance from the dwarf, and, after resting for a time, it began to eat the berries and to throw the stones into the lake, and wherever a stone fell a bright red stain appeared in the water. As he looked more closely at the bird the dwarf saw that it had all the signs of old age, and he could not help wondering how it was able to carry such a heavy tree.

Later in the day, two other birds, as large as the first, but younger, came up from the west and settled down beside him. They also ate the berries, and throwing the stones into the lake it was soon as red as wine.

When they had eaten all the berries, the young birds began to pick the decayed feathers off the old bird and to smooth his plumage. As soon as they had completed their task, he rose slowly from the hill and sailed out over the lake, and dropping down on the waters, dived beneath them. In a moment he came to the surface, and shot up into the air with a joyous cry, and flew off to the west in all the vigour of renewed youth, followed by the

15

other birds.

When they had gone so far that they were like specks in the sky, the dwarf mounted his horse and descended towards the lake.

He was almost at the margin, and in other minute would have plunged in, when he heard a fierce screaming in the air, and before he had time to look up, the three birds were hovering over the lake.

The dwarf drew back frightened.

The birds wheeled over his head, and then, swooping down, they flew close to the water, covering it with their wings, and uttering harsh cries.

Then, rising to a great height, they folded their wings and dropped headlong, like three rocks, on the lake, crashing its surface, and scattering a wine-red shower upon the hills.[1]

Then the dwarf remembered what the fairy told him, that if he attempted to swim the lake, without paying the price, the three Cormorants of the Western Seas would pick the flesh off his bones. He knew not what to do, and was about to turn away, when he heard once more the twang of the golden harp, and the little fairy of the hills stood before him.

'Faint heart never won fair lady,' said the little harper. 'Are you ready to pay the price? The spear and shield are on the opposite bank, and the Princess Finola is crying this moment in the lonely moor.'

At the mention of Finola's name the dwarf's heart grew strong.

'Yes,' he said; 'I am ready — win or die. What is the price?'

'Your left eye,' said the fairy. And as soon as said he scooped out the eye, and put it in his pocket.

The poor blind dwarf almost fainted with pain.

'It's your last trial,' said the fairy, 'and now do what I tell you. Twist your horse's mane round your right hand, and I will lead him to the water. Plunge in, and fear not. I gave you back your speech. When you reach the opposite bank you will get back your memory, and you will know who and what you are.'

Then the fairy led the horse to the margin of the lake.

'In with you now, and good luck go with you,' said the fairy.

The dwarf urged the horse. He plunged into the lake, and went down and down until his feet struck the bottom. Then he began to ascend, and as he came near the surface of the water the dwarf thought he saw a glimmering light, and when he rose above the water he saw the bright sun shining and the green hills before him, and he shouted with joy at finding his sight restored.

But he saw more. Instead of the old horse he had ridden into the lake he was bestride a noble steed, and as the steed swam to the bank the dwarf felt a change coming over himself, and an unknown vigour in his limbs.

When the steed touched the shore he galloped up the hillside, and on the top of the hill was a silver shield, bright as the sun, resting against a spear standing upright in the ground.

The dwarf jumped off, and, running towards the shield, he saw himself as in a looking-glass.

He was no longer a dwarf, but a gallant knight. At that moment his memory came back to him, and he knew he was Conal, one of the Knights of the Red Branch, and he remembered now that the spell of dumbness and deformity had been cast upon him by the Witch of the Palace of the Quicken Trees.

Slinging his shield upon his left arm, he plucked the spear from the ground and leaped on to his horse. With a light heart he swam back over the lake, and nowhere could he see the black Cormorants of the Western Sea, but three white swans floating abreast followed him to the bank. When he reached the bank he galloped down to the sea, and crossed to the shore.

Then he flung the reins upon his horse's neck, and swifter than the wind the gallant horse swept on and on, and it was not long before he was bounding over the enchanted moor. Wherever his hoofs struck the ground, grass and flowers sprang up, and great trees with leafy branches rose on every side.

At last the knight reached the little hut. Three times he struck the shield with the haft and three times with the blade of his spear. At the last blow the hut disappeared, and standing before him was the little princess.

The knight took her in his arms and kissed her; then he lifted her onto the horse, and, leaping up before her, he turned towards the north, to the palace of the Red Branch Knights, and as they rode on beneath the leafy trees from every tree the birds sang out, for the spell of silence over the lonely moor was broken for ever.

THE HOUSE IN THE LAKE[2]

A long, long time ago there lived in a little hut, in the midst of one of the inland lakes of Erin, an old fisherman and his son. The hut was built on stakes driven into the bed of the lake, and was so high above the waters that even when they were stirred into waves by the wind coming down from the mountains they did not reach the threshold of the door. Around, outside the hut, on a level with the floor, was a little wicker-work platform, and under the platform, close to the steps leading up to it from the water, the fisherman's curragh, made of willows, covered with skins, was moored, and it was only by means of the curragh that he and his son, Enda, could leave their lake dwelling.

On many a summer evening Enda lay stretched on the platform, watching the sunset fading from the mountain-tops, and the twilight creeping over the waters of the lake, and it chanced that once when he was so engaged he heard a rustle in a clump of sedge that grew close to one side of the hut. He turned to where the sound came from, and what should he see but an otter swimming towards him, with a little trout in his mouth. When the otter came up to where Enda was lying, he lifted his head and half his body from the water, and flung the trout on the platform, almost at Enda's feet, and then disappeared.

Enda took the little panting trout in his hand; but as he did so he heard, quite close to him, in the lake, a sound like that of water splashing upon water, and he saw the widening circles caused by a trout which had just risen to a fly; and he said to the little trout he held in his hand:

'I won't keep you, poor thing! Perhaps that was a little comrade come to look for you, and so I'll send you back to him.'

And saying this, he dropped the little trout into the lake.

Well, when the next evening came, again Enda was lying stretched outside the hut, and once more he heard the rustle in the sedge, and once more the otter came and flung the little trout almost into his hands.

Enda, more surprised than ever, did not know what to do. He saw that it was the same little trout the otter had brought him the night before, and he said:

'Well, I gave you a chance last night. I'll give you another, if only to see what will come of it.'

And he dropped the trout into the lake; but no sooner had it touched the waters than it was changed into a beautiful, milk-white swan. And Enda could hardly believe his eyes, as he saw it sailing across the lake, until it was lost in the sedges growing by the shore.

All that night he lay awake, thinking of what he had seen, and as soon as the morning stood on the hill-tops, and cast its shafts of golden light across the lake, Enda rose and got into his curragh.

He rowed all round the shores, beating the sedges with his oar, in pursuit of the swan; but all in vain; he could not catch a glimpse of her white plumage anywhere. Day after day he rowed about the lake in search of her, and every evening he lay outside the hut watching the waters. At long last, one night, when the full moon, rising above the mountains, flooded the whole lake with light, he saw the swan coming swiftly towards him, shining brighter than the moonbeams. The swan came on until it was almost within a boat's length of the hut; and what should Enda hear but the swam speaking to him in his own language:

'Get into your curragh, Enda, and follow me,' said she, and, saying this, she turned round and sailed away.

Enda jumped into the curragh, and soon the water, dripping from his oar, was flashing like diamonds in the moonlight. And he rowed after the swan, who glided on before him, until she came to where the shadows of the mountains lay deepest on the lake. Then the swan rested, and when Enda came up to her:

'Enda,' said she, 'I have brought you where none may hear what I wish to say to you. I am Mave, the daughter of the king of Erin. By the magic arts of my cruel stepmother I was changed into a trout, and cast into this lake a year and a day before the evening when you restored me to the waters the second time. If you had not done so the first night the otter brought me to you I should have been changed into a hooting owl; if you had not done so the second night, I should have been changed into a croaking raven. But, thanks to you, Enda, I am now a snow-white swan, and for one hour on the first night of every full moon the power of speech is and will be given to me as long as I remain a swan. And a swan I must always remain, unless you are willing to break the spell of enchantment that is over me; and you alone can break it.'

21

'I'll do anything I can for you, O princess!' said Enda. 'But how can I break the spell?'

'You can do so,' said the swan, 'only by pouring upon my plumage the perfumed water that fills the golden bowl that is in the inmost room of the palace of the fairy queen, beneath the lake.'

'And how can I get that?' said Enda.

'Well,' said the swan, 'you must dive beneath the lake, and walk along its bed, until you come to where the lake dragon guards the entrance of the fairy queen's dominions.'

'I can dive like a fish,' said Enda; 'but how can I walk beneath the waters?'

'You can do it easily enough,' said the sawn, 'if you get the water-dress of Brian, one of the tree sons of Turenn, and his helmet of transparent crystal, by the aid of which he was able to walk under the green salt sea.'[3]

'And where shall I find them?'

'They are in the water-palace of Angus of the Boyne,' said the swan; 'but you should set out at once, for if the spell be not broken before the moon is full again, it cannot be broken for a year and a day.'

'I'll set out in the first ray of the morning,' said Enda.

'May luck and joy go with you,' said the swan. 'And now the hours of silence are coming upon me, and I have only time to warn you that dangers you little dream of will lie before you in your quest for the golden cup.'

'I am willing to face all dangers for your sake, O princess,' said Enda.

'Blessings be upon you, Enda,' said the swan, and she sailed away from the shadow out into the light across the lake to the sedgy banks. And Enda saw her no more.

He rowed his curragh home, and he lay on his bed without taking off his clothes. And as the first faint glimmer of the morning came slanting down the mountains, he stepped into his curragh and pulled across the lake, and took the road towards the water-place of Angus of the Boyne.

When he reached the banks of the glancing river a little woman, dressed in red, was standing there before him.

'You are welcome, Enda,' said she. 'And glad am I to see the day that brings you here to help the winsome Princess Mave. And now wait a second, and the water-dress and crystal helmet will be ready for you.'

And, having said this, the little woman plucked a handful of wild grasses, and she breathed upon them three times and then flung them on the river, and a dozen fairy nymphs came springing up through the water, bearing the water-dress and crystal helmet and a shining spear. And they laid them down upon the bank at Enda's feet, and then disappeared.

'Now, Enda,' said the fairy woman, 'take these; by the aid of the dress and the helmet you can walk beneath the waters. You will need the spear to enable you to meet the dangers that lie before you. But with that spear, if you only have courage, you can overcome everything and everyone that may attempt to bar your way.'

Having said this, she bid good-bye to Enda, and stepping off the bank, she floated out upon the river as lightly as a red poppy leaf. And when she came to the middle of the stream she disappeared beneath the waters.

Enda took the helmet, dress, and spear, and it was not long until he came to the sedgy banks where his little boat was waiting for him. As he stepped into the curragh the moon was rising above the mountains. He rowed on until he came to the hut, and having moored the boat to the door, he put on the water-dress and the crystal helmet, and taking the spear in his hand, he leaped over the side of the curragh, and sank down and down until he touched the bottom. Then he walked along without minding where he was going, and the only light he had was the shimmering moonlight, which descended as faintly through the waters as if it came through muffled glass. He had not gone very far when he heard a horrible hissing, and straight before him he saw what he thought were two flaming coals. After a few more steps he found himself face to face with the dragon of the lake, the guardian of the palace of the fairy queen. Before he had time to raise his spear, the dragon had wound its coils around him, and he heard its horrible teeth crunching against the side of his crystal helmet, and he felt the pressure of its coils around his side, and the breath almost left his body; but the dragon, unable to pierce the helmet, unwound his coils, and soon Enda's hands were free, and before the dragon could attempt to seize him again, he drove his spear through one of its fiery eyes, and, writhing with pain, the hissing dragon darted through a cave behind him. Enda, gaining courage from the dragon's flight, marched on until he came to a door of dull brass set in the rocks. He tried to push it in before him, but he might as well have tried to push away the rocks.

While he was wondering what he should do, he heard again the fierce hissing of the dragon, and saw the red glare of his fiery eye dimly in the water.

Lifting his spear and hastily turning round to meet the furious monster, Enda accidently touched the door with the point of the spear, and the door flew open. Enda passed through, and the door closed behind him with a grating sound, and he marched along through a rocky pass which led to a sandy plain.

As he stepped from the pass into the plain the sands began to move, as if they were alive. In a second a thousand hideous serpents, almost the colour of the sand, rose hissing up, and with their forked tongues made a horrible, poisonous hedge in front of him. For a second he stood dismayed, but then, levelling his spear, he rushed against the hedge of serpents, and they, shooting poison at him, sank beneath the sand. But the poison did not harm him, because of his water-dress and crystal helmet.

When he had passed over the sandy plain, he had to climb a great steep, jagged rock. When he got to the top of the rock he saw spread out before him a stony waste without a tuft or blade of grass. At some distance in front of him he noticed a large dark object, which he took to be a rock, but on looking at it more closely he saw that it was a huge, misshapen, swollen mass, apparently alive. And it was growing bigger and bigger every moment. Enda stood amazed at the sight, and before he knew where he was the loathsome creature rose from the ground, and sprang upon him before he could use his spear, and, catching him in its horrid grasp, flung him back over the rocks onto the sandy plain. Enda was almost stunned, but the hissing of the serpents rising from the sand around him brought him to himself, and, jumping to his feet, once more he drove them down beneath the surface. He then approached the jagged rock, on the top of which he saw the filthy monster glaring at him with bloodshot eyes. Enda poised his spear and hurled it against his enemy. It entered between the monster's eyes, and from the wound the blood flowed down like a black torrent and dyed the plain, and the shrunken carcass slipped down the front of the rocks and disappeared beneath the sand. Enda once more ascended the rock, and without meeting or seeing anything he passed over the stony waste, and at last he came to a leafy wood. He had not gone far in the wood until he heard the sound of fairy music, and walking on he came upon a mossy glade, and there he found the fairies dancing around their queen. They were so small, and were all so brightly dressed, that they looked like a mass of wavering flowers; but when he was seen by them they vanished like a glorious dream, and no one remained before him but the fairy queen. The queen blushed at finding herself alone, but on stamping her little foot three times upon the ground, the frightened fairies all crept back again.

'You are welcome, Enda,' said the queen. 'My little subjects have been alarmed by your strange dress and crystal helmet. I pray you take them off; you do not need them here.'

Enda did as he was bidden, and he laid down his water-dress and the helmet on the grass, and the little fairies, seeing him in his proper shape, got over their fright, and, unrestrained by the presence of the queen, they ran tumbling over one another to try and get a good look at the crystal helmet.

'I know what you have come for, Enda,' said the queen. 'The golden cup you shall have tomorrow; but tonight you must share our feast, so follow me to the palace.'

Having said this, the queen beckoned her pages to her, and, attended by them and followed by Enda, she went on through the wood. When they had left it behind them Enda saw on a green hill before him the snow-white palace of the fairy queen.

As the queen approached the steps that led up to the open door, a band of tiny fairies, dressed in rose-coloured silk, came out, carrying baskets of flowers, which they flung down on the steps to make a fragrant carpet for her. They were followed by a band of harpers dressed in yellow silken robes, who ranged themselves on each side of the steps and played their sweetest music as the queen ascended.

When the queen, followed by Enda, entered the palace, they passed through a crystal hall that led to a banquet-room. The room was lighted by a single star, large as a battle-shield. It was fixed against the wall above a diamond throne.

The queen seated herself upon the throne, and the pages, advancing towards her, and bending low, as they approached the steps, handed her a golden wand.

The queen waved the wand three times, and a table laden with all kinds of delicacies appeared upon the floor. Then she beckoned Enda to her, and when he stood beside her the fairy table was no higher than his knee.

'I am afraid I must make you smaller, Enda,'

said the queen, 'or you will never be able to seat yourself at my fairy table.'

And having said this, she touched Enda with the golden wand, and at once he became as small as her tallest page. Then she struck the steps of her throne, and all the nobles of her court, headed by her bards, took their places at the festive board.

The feast went on right merrily, and when the tiny jewelled drinking-cups were placed upon the table, the queen ordered the harpers to play.

And the little harpers struck the chords, and as Enda listened to the music it seemed to him as if he was being slowly lifted from his seat, and when the music ended the fairies vanished, the shining star went out, and Enda was in perfect darkness.

The air blew keenly in his face, and he knew not where he was. At last he saw a faint grey light, and soon this light grew broader and brighter, and as the shadows fled before it, he could hardly believe his eyes when he found himself in his curragh on the lake, and the moonlight streaming down from the mountain-tops.

For a moment he thought he must have been dreaming; but there in the boat before him were the crystal helmet, and the water-dress, and the gleaming spear, and the golden bowl of perfumed water that was to remove the spell of enchantment from the white swan of the lake, and sailing towards him from the sedgy bank came the snow-white swan; and when she touched the boat, Enda put out his hands and lifted her in, and then over her plumage he poured the perfumed water from the golden bowl, and the Princess Mave in all her maiden beauty stood before him.

'Take your oar, Enda,' she said, 'and row to the

southern bank.'

Enda seized his oar, and the curragh sped across the waters swifter than a swallow in its flight. When the boat touched the shore Enda jumped out, and lifted the princess to the bank.

'Send your boat adrift, Enda,' she said; 'but first take out your shining spear; the water-dress and the crystal helmet will take care of themselves.'

Enda took out the spear, and then pushed the boat from the bank. It sped on towards the hut in the middle of the lake; but before it had reached halfway six nymphs sprang up from the water and seizing the helmet and dress, sank with them beneath the tide, and the boat went on until it pushed its prow against the steps of the little hut, where it remained.

Then Enda and the princess turned towards the south, and it was not long until they came to a deep forest, that was folding up its shadows and spreading out its mossy glades before the glancing footsteps of the morning. They had not gone far through the forest when they heard the music of hounds and the cries of huntsmen, and crashing towards them through the low branches they saw a fierce wild boar. Enda, gently pushing the princess behind him, levelled his spear, and when the boar came close to him he drove it into his throat. The brute fell dead at his feet, and the dogs rushing up began to tear it to pieces. The princess fainted at the sight, and while Enda was endeavouring to restore her, the king of Erin, followed by his huntsmen, appeared, and when the king saw the princess he started in amazement, as he recognised the features of his daughter Mave.

At that moment the princess came to herself and

her father, lifting her tenderly in his arms, kissed her again and again.

'I have mourned you as dead, my darling,' said he, 'and now you are restored to me more lovely than ever. I would gladly have given up my throne for this. But say who is the champion who has brought you hither, and who has slain the wild boar we have hunted so many years in vain?'

The princess blushed like a rose as she said:

'His name is Enda, father; it is he has brought me back to you.'

Then the king embraced Enda and said:

'Forgive me, Enda, for asking any questions about you before you have shared the hospitality of my court. My palace lies beyond the forest, and we shall reach it soon.'

Then the king ordered his huntsman to sound the bugle-horn, and all his nobles galloped up in answer to it, and when they saw the Princess Mave they were so dazzled by her beauty that they scarcely gave a thought to the death of the wild boar.

'It is my daughter, Mave, come back to me,' said the king.

And all the nobles lowered their lances, and bowed in homage to the lady.

'And there stands the champion who has brought her home,' said the king, pointing to Enda.

The nobles looked and Enda, and bowed courteously, but in their hearts they were jealous of the champion, for they saw he was already a favourite of the king's.

Then the pages came up, leading milk-white steeds with golden bridles, and the king, ordering Enda to mount one of them, lifted Mave on to his

30

own, and mounted behind her. The pages, carrying the boar's head on a hollow shield, preceded by the huntsmen sounding their horns, set out towards the palace, and the royal party followed them.

As the procession approached the palace crowds came rushing out to see the trophies of the chase, and through the snow-white door the queen, Mave's cruel stepmother, attended by her maids-of-honour and the royal bards, came forth to greet the king. But when she saw seated before him the Princess Mave, who she thought was at the bottom of the lake under a spell of enchantment, she uttered a loud cry, and fell senseless to the ground.

The king jumped from his horse, and rushing to the queen, lifted her up and carried her in his arms to her apartments, for he had no suspicion of the wickedness of which she had been guilty.

And the court leeches were summoned to attend her, but she died that very night, and it was not until a green mound, worthy of a queen of Erin, had been raised over her grave that Princess Mave told her father of the wickedness of her step-mother. And when she told him the whole story of how Enda had broken the spell of enchantment and of the dangers which he had faced for her sake, the king summoned an assembly of all his nobles, and seated on his throne, wearing his golden helmet, the bards upon his right hand and the Druids upon his left, and the nobles in ranks before him with gleaming helmets and flashing spears, he told them the story of the princess, and of the service which Enda had rendered to her.

'And now,' said the king, 'if the princess is willing to take her deliverer for her husband, I am willing that she shall be his bride; and if you, my subjects, bards and Druids and nobles and chiefs of Erin, have anything to say against this union, speak. But first, Mave,' said the king, as he drew the blushing princess to him, 'speak, darling, as becomes the daughter of a king — speak in the presence of the nobles of Erin, and say if it is your wish to become Enda's bride.'

The princess flung her white arms around her father's neck, as she murmured:

'Father, it was Enda brought me back to you, and before all the princes and nobles of Erin I am willing to be his bride.'

And she buried her head upon the king's breast, and as he stroked her silken hair falling to her feet, the bards struck their golden harps, but the sound of the joyous music could hardly drown the murmurs of the jealous nobles.

When the music ceased the king beckoned Enda to him, and was about to place his hand in Mave's when a Druid, whose white beard almost touched the ground, and who had been a favourite of the dead stepmother, and hated Mave for her sake, stepped forward and said:

'O King of Erin, never yet has the daughter of a king been freely given in marriage to any save a battle champion; and that stripling there has never struck his spear against a warrior's shield.'

A murmur of approbation rose from the jealous princes, and Congal, the bravest of them all, stepped out from the ranks, and said:

'The Druid speaks the truth, O king! That stripling has never faced a battle champion yet, and, speaking for all the nobles of your land, I challenge him to fight any one of us; and as he is young and unused to arms, we are willing that the youngest and least experienced among us should be set against him.'

When Congal had spoken, the nobles, in approval of his words, struck their shields with their swords, and the brazen sound ascended to the skies.

The face of the princess, blushing a moment before like a rose, became as white as a lily; but the colour returned to her cheeks when she heard Enda's voice ringing loud and clear.

'It is true, O king!' said he, 'that I have never used my spear in battle yet. The Prince Congal has challenged me to meet the youngest and least experienced of the chiefs of Erin. I have risked my life already for your daughter's sake. I would face death a thousand times for the chance of winning her for my bride; but I would scorn to claim her hand if I dared not meet the boldest battle champion of the nobles of Erin, and here before you, O king, and bards, Druids, and nobles, and chiefs of Erin, and her, in the presence of the Lady Mave, I challenge the boldest of them all.'

The king's eyes flashed with joy as he listened to the brave words of Enda.

'It is well,' said the king; 'the contest shall take place tomorrow on the lawn outside our palace gates; but before our assembly dissolves I call on you, nobles and chiefs of Erin, to name your boldest champion.'

Loud cries of 'Congal! Congal!' answered the king's speech.

'Are you willing, Congal?' asked the king.

'Willing, O king!' answered Congal.

'It is well,' said the king. 'We shall all meet again tonight in our banquet-hall.'

And the king, with the Princess Mave on his arm,

attended by his bards and Druids, entered the palace, and the chiefs and nobles went their several ways.

At the feast that night the princess sat beside the king, and Enda beside the princess, and the bards and Druids, nobles and chiefs, took their places in due order. And the bards sang songs of love and battle, and never merrier hours were spent than those which passed away that night in the banquet-hall of Erin's king.

When the feast was over Enda retired to his apartment to spend the night dreaming of the Princess Mave, and Congal went to his quarters; but not to sleep or dream, for the Druid who had provoked the contest came to him bringing his golden wand, and all night long the Druid was weaving spells to charm the shield and spear and helmet of Congal, to make them invulnerable in the battle of the morrow.

But while Enda lay dreaming of the Princess Mave, the little fairy woman who gave him the water-dress, and the crystal helmet, and shining spear on the banks of the Boyne, slid into his room, and she placed beside his couch a silver helmet and a silver shield. And she rubbed the helmet, and the shield, and the blue blade and haft of his spear with the juice of the red rowan berries, and she let a drop fall upon his face and hands, and then she slid out as silently as she came.

When the morning broke, Enda sprang from his couch, and he could hardly believe his eyes when he saw the silver shield and helmet. At the sight of them he longed for the hour of battle, and he watched with eager gaze the sun climbing the sky; and, after hours of suspense, he heard the trumpet's sound and the clangour of the hollow shields, struck by the hard-pointed spears.

Putting on the helmet, and fastening the shield upon his left arm, and taking the spear in his right hand, he stepped out bravely to the fight. The edge of the lawn before the palace gates was ringed by the princes, nobles, and chiefs of Erin. And the palace walls were thronged by all the beauties of the Court and all the noble ladies of the land. And on his throne, surrounded by his Druids, his brehons, and his bards, was the king of Erin, and at his feet sat the lovely Lady Mave.

As Enda stepped out upon the lawn, he saw Congal advancing from the ranks of the nobles, and the two champions approached each other until they met right in front of the throne.

Then both turned towards the throne, and bowed to the king and the Princess Mave; and then facing each other again, they retired a space, and when their spears were poised, ready for battle, the king gave the signal, which was answered by the clang of stricken shields, and Congal and Enda launched their gleaming spears. They flashed like lightning in the sunlit air, and in a second Congal's had broken against Enda's shield; but Enda's, piercing Congal's helmet, hurled him senseless on the plain.

The nobles and chiefs could hardly realise that in that single second their boldest champion was overthrown; but when they saw him stretched motionless on the grassy sward, from out their ranks six warriors advanced to where the chieftain lay, and sadly they bore him away upon their battle-shields, and Enda remained victor upon the field.

And then the king's voice rang out clear as the sound of a trumpet in the still morning:

'Bards and brehons, princes and nobles, and chiefs of Erin, Enda has proved himself a battle champion, and who amongst you now will dare gainsay his right to claim my daughter for his bride?'

And no answer came.

But when he summoned Enda to his throne, and placed the lady's hand in his, a cheer arose from the great assembly, that proved that jealousy was extinguished in all hearts, and that all believed that Enda was worthy of the winsome bride; and never since that day, although a thousand years have passed, was there in all the world a brighter and gayer wedding than the wedding of Enda and the Princess Mave.

THE LITTLE WHITE CAT

A long, long time ago, in a valley far away, the giant Trencoss lived in a great castle, surrounded by trees that were always green. The castle had a hundred doors, and every door was guarded by a huge, shaggy hound, with tongue of fire and claws of iron, who tore to pieces anyone who went to the castle without the giant's leave. Trencoss had made war on the King of the Torrents, and, having killed the king, and slain his people, and burned his palace, he carried off his only daughter, the Princess Eileen, to the castle in the valley. Here he provided her with beautiful rooms, and appointed a hundred dwarfs, dressed in blue and yellow satin, to wait upon her, and harpers to play sweet music for her, and he gave her diamonds without number, brighter than the sun; but he would not allow her to go outside the castle, and told her if she went one step beyond its doors, the hounds, with tongues of fire and claws of iron, would tear her to pieces. A week after her arrival, war broke out between the giant and the king of the islands, and before he set out for battle, the giant sent for the princess, and informed her that on his return he would make her his wife. When the princess heard this she began to cry, for she would rather die than marry the giant who had slain her father.

'Crying will only spoil your bright eyes, my little princess,' said Trencoss, 'and you will have to marry me whether you like it or no.'

He then bade her go back to her room, and he ordered the dwarfs to give her everything she asked for while he was away, and the harpers to play the sweetest music for her. When the princess gained her room she cried as if her heart would break. The long day passed slowly, and the night came, but brought no sleep to Eileen, and in the grey light of the morning she rose and opened the window, and looked about in every direction to see if there were any chance of escape. But the window was ever so high above the ground, and below were the hungry and ever watchful hounds. With a heavy heart she was about to close the window when she thought she saw the branches of the tree that was nearest to it moving. She looked again, and she saw a little white cat creeping along one of the branches.

'Mew!' cried the cat.

'Poor little pussy,' said the princess. 'Come to me, pussy.'

'Stand back from the window,' said the cat, 'and I will.'

The princess stepped back, and the little white cat jumped into the room. The princess took the little cat on her lap and stroked him with her hand, and the cat raised its back and began to purr.

'Where do you come from, and what is your name?' asked the princess.

'No matter where I come from or what's my name?' said the cat. 'I am a friend of yours, and I come to help you?'

'I never wanted help worse,' said the princess.

'I know that,' said the cat; 'and now listen to me. When the giant comes back from battle and asks you to marry him, say to him you will marry him.'

'But I will never marry him,' said the princess.

'Do what I tell you,' said the cat. 'When he asks you to marry him, say to him you will if his dwarfs will wind for you three balls from the fairy dew that lies on the bushes on a misty morning as big as these,' said the cat, putting his right forefoot into his ear and taking out three balls — one yellow, one red, and one blue.

'They are very small,' said the princess. 'They are not much bigger than peas, and the dwarfs will not be long at their work.'

'Won't they,' said the cat. 'It will take them a month and a day to make one, so that it will take three months and three days before the balls are wound; but the giant, like you, will think they can be made in a few days, and so he will readily promise to do what you ask. He will soon find out his mistake, but he will keep his word, and will not press you to marry him until the balls are wound.'

'When will the giant come back?' asked Eileen.

'He will return tomorrow afternoon,' said the cat.

'Will you stay with me until then?' said the princess. 'I am very lonely.'

'I cannot stay,' said the cat. 'I have to go away to my palace on the island on which no man ever placed his foot, and where no man but one shall ever come.'

'And where is that island?' asked the princess, 'and who is the man?'

'The island is in the far-off seas where vessel never sailed; the man you will see before many days are over; and if all goes well, he will one day slay the giant Trencoss, and free you from his power.'

'Ah!' sighed the princess, 'that can never be, for

no weapon can wound the hundred hounds that guard the castle, and no sword can kill the giant Trencoss.'

'There is a sword that will kill him,' said the cat; 'but I must go now. Remember what you are to say to the giant when he comes home, and every morning watch the tree on which you saw me, and if you see in the branches anyone you like better than yourself,' said the cat, winking at the princess, 'throw him these three balls and leave the rest to me; but take care not to speak a single word to him, for if you do all will be lost.'

'Shall I ever see you again?' asked the princess.

'Time will tell,' answered the cat, and, without saying so much as good-bye, he jumped through the window onto the tree, and in a second was out of sight.

The morrow afternoon came, and the giant Trencoss returned from battle. Eileen knew of his coming by the furious barking of the hounds, and her heart sank, for she knew that in a few moments she would be summoned to his presence. Indeed, he had hardly entered the castle when he sent for her, and told her to get ready for the wedding. The princess tried to look cheerful, as she answered:

'I will be ready as soon as you wish; but you must first promise me something.'

'Ask anything you like, little princess,' said Trencoss.

'Well, then,' said Eileen, 'before I marry you, you must make your dwarfs wind three balls as big as these from the fairy dew that lies on the bushes on a misty morning in summer.'

'Is that all?' said Trencoss, laughing. 'I shall give the dwarfs orders at once, and by this time tomorrow the balls will be wound, and our wedding can take place in the evening.'

'And will you leave me to myself until then?'

'I will,' said Trencoss.

'On your honour as a giant?' said Eileen.

'On my honour as a giant,' replied Trencoss.

The princess returned to her rooms, and the giant summoned all his dwarfs, and he ordered them to go forth in the dawning of the morn and to gather all the fairy dew lying on the bushes, and to wind three balls — one yellow, one red, and one blue. The next morning, and the next, and the next, the dwarfs went out into the fields and searched all the hedgerows, but they could gather only as much fairy dew as would make a thread as long as a wee girl's eyelash; and so they had to go out morning after morning, and the giant fumed and threatened, but all to no purpose. He was very angry with the princess, and he was vexed with himself that she was so much cleverer than he was, and, moreover, he saw now that the wedding could not take place as soon as he expected.

When the little white cat went away from the castle he ran as fast as he could up hill and down dale, and never stopped until he came to the Prince of the Silver River. The prince was alone, and very sad and sorrowful he was, for he was thinking of the Princess Eileen, and wondering where she could be.

'Mew,' said the cat, as he sprang softly into the room; but the prince did not heed him. 'Mew,' again said the cat; but again the prince did not heed him. 'Mew,' said the cat the third time, and he jumped up on the prince's knee.

'Where do you come from, and what do you want?' asked the prince.

41

'I come from where you would like to be,' said the cat.

'And where is that?' said the prince.

'Oh, where is that, indeed! as if I didn't know what you are thinking of, and of whom you are thinking,' said the cat; 'and it would be far better for you to try and save her.'

'I would give my life a thousand times over for her,' said the prince.

'For whom?' said the cat, with a wink. 'I named no name, your highness,' said he.

'You know very well who she is,' said the prince, 'if you knew what I was thinking of; but do you know where she is?'

'She is in danger,' said the cat. 'She is in the castle of the giant Trencoss, in the valley beyond the mountains.'

'I will set out there at once,' said the prince, 'and I will challenge the giant to battle, and will slay him.'

'Easier said than done,' said the cat. 'There is no sword made by the hands of man can kill him, and even if you could kill him, his hundred hounds, with tongues of fire and claws of iron, would tear you to pieces.'

'Then, what am I to do?' asked the prince.

'Be said by me,' said the cat. 'Go to the wood that surrounds the giant's castle, and climb the high tree that's nearest to the window that looks towards the sunset, and shake the branches, and you will see what you will see. Then hold out your hat with the silver plumes, and three balls — one yellow, one red, and one blue — will be thrown into it. And then come back here as fast as you can; but speak no word, for if you utter a single word the hounds will hear you, and you shall be torn to pieces.'

Well, the prince set off at once, and after two days' journey he came to the wood around the castle, and he climbed the tree that was nearest to the window that looked towards the sunset, and he shook the branches. As soon as he did so, the window opened and he saw the Princess Eileen, looking lovelier than ever. He was going to call out her name, but she placed her fingers on her lips, and he remembered what the cat had told him, that he was to speak no word. In silence he held out the hat with the silver plumes, and the princess threw into it the three balls, one after another, and, blowing him a kiss, she shut the window. And well it was she did so, for at that very moment she heard the voice of the giant, who was coming back from hunting.

The prince waited until the giant had entered the castle before he descended the tree. He set off as fast as he could. He went up hill and down dale, and never stopped until he arrived at his own palace, and there waiting for him was the little white cat.

'Have you brought the three balls?' said he.

'I have,' said the prince.

'Then follow me,' said the cat.

On they went until they left the palace far behind and came to the edge of the sea.

'Now,' said the cat, 'unravel a thread of the red ball, hold the thread in your right hand, drop the ball into the water, and you shall see what you shall see.'

The prince did as he was told, and the ball floated out to sea, unravelling as it went, and it went on until it was out of sight.

'Pull now,' said the cat.

The prince pulled, and, as he did, he saw far away something on the sea shining like silver. It came nearer and nearer, and he saw it was a little silver boat. At last it touched the sand.

'Now,' said the cat, 'step into this boat and it will bear you to the palace on the island on which no man has ever placed his foot — the island in the unknown seas that were never sailed by vessels made of human hands. In that palace there is a sword with a diamond hilt, and by that sword alone the giant Trencoss can be killed. There also are a hundred cakes, and it is only on eating these the hundred hounds can die. But mind what I say to you: if you eat or drink until you reach the palace of the little cat in the island in the unknown seas, you will forget the Princess Eileen.'

'I will forget myself first,' said the prince, as he stepped into the silver boat, which floated away so quickly that it was soon out of sight of land.

The day passed and the night fell, and the stars shone down upon the waters, but the boat never stopped. On she went for two whole days and nights, and on the third morning the prince saw an island in the distance, and very glad he was; for he thought it was his journey's end, and he was almost fainting with thirst and hunger. But the day passed and the island was still before him.

At long last, on the following day, he saw by the first light of the morning that he was quite close to it, and that trees laden with fruit of every kind were bending down over the water. The boat sailed round and round the island, going closer and closer every round, until, at last, the drooping branches

44

almost touched it. The sight of the fruit within his reach made the prince hungrier and thirstier than he was before, and forgetting his promise to the little cat — not to eat anything until he entered the palace in the unknown seas — he caught one of the branches, and, in a moment, was in the tree eating the delicious fruit. While he was doing so the boat floated out to sea and soon was lost to sight; but the prince, having eaten, forgot all about it, and, worse still, forgot all about the princess in the giant's castle. When he had eaten enough he descended the tree, and, turning his back on the sea, set out straight before him. He had not gone far when he heard the sound of music, and soon after he saw a number of maidens playing on silver harps coming towards him. When they saw him they ceased playing, and cried out:

'Welcome! welcome! Prince of the Silver River, welcome to the island of fruits and flowers. Our king and queen saw you coming over the sea, and they sent us to bring you to the palace.'

The prince went with them, and at the palace gates the king and queen and their daughter Kathleen received him, and gave him welcome. He hardly saw the king and queen, for his eyes were fixed on the Princess Kathleen, who looked more beautiful than a flower. He thought he had never seen anyone so lovely, for, of course, he had forgotten all about poor Eileen pining away in her castle prison in the lonely valley. When the king and queen had given welcome to the prince a great feast was spread, and all the lords and ladies of the court sat down to it, and the prince sat between the queen and the Princess Kathleen, and long before the feast was finished he was over head and ears in love with her. When the feast was ended the queen ordered the ballroom to be made ready, and when night fell the dancing began, and was kept up until the morning star, and the prince danced all night with the princess, falling deeper and deeper in love with her every minute. Between dancing by night and feasting by day weeks went by. All the time poor Eileen in the giant's castle was counting the hours, and all this time the dwarfs were winding the balls, and a ball and a half were already wound. At last the prince asked the king and queen for their daughter in marriage, and they were delighted to be able to say yes, and the day was fixed for the wedding. But on the evening before the day on which it was to take place the prince was in his room, getting ready for a dance, when he felt something rubbing against his leg. and, looking down, who should he see but the little white cat. At the sight of him the prince remembered everything, and sad and sorry he was when he thought of Eileen watching and waiting and counting the days until he returned to save her. But he was very fond of the Princess Kathleen, and so he did not know what to do.

'You can't do anything tonight,' said the cat, for he knew what the prince was thinking of, 'but when morning comes go down to the sea, and look not to the right or the left, and let no living thing touch you, for if you do you shall never leave the island. Drop the second ball into the water, as you did the first, and when the boat comes step in at once. Then you may look behind you, and you shall see what you shall see, and you'll know which you love best, the Princess Eileen or the Princess Kathleen, and you can either go or stay.

46

The prince didn't sleep a wink that night, and at the first glimpse of the morning he stole from the palace. When he reached the sea he threw out the ball, and when it had floated out of sight, he saw the little boat sparkling on the horizon like a newly-risen star. The prince had scarcely passed through the palace doors when he was missed, and the king and queen and the princess, and all the lords and ladies of the court, went in search of him, taking the quickest way to the sea. While the maidens with the silver harps played sweetest music, the princess, whose voice was sweeter than any music, called on the prince by his name, and so moved his heart that he was about to look behind, when he remembered how the cat had told him that he should not do so until he was in the boat. Just as it touched the shore the princess put out her hand and almost caught the prince's arm, but he stepped into the boat in time to save himself, and it sped away like a receding wave. A loud scream caused the prince to look round suddenly, and when he did he saw no sign of king or queen, or princess, or lords or ladies, but only big green serpents, with red eyes and tongues, that hissed out fire and poison as they writhed in a hundred horrible coils.

The prince, having escaped from the enchanted island, sailed away for three days and three nights, and every night he hoped the coming morning would show him the island he was in search of. He was faint with hunger and beginning to despair, when on the fourth morning he saw in the distance an island that, in the first rays of the sun, gleamed like fire. On coming closer to it he saw that it was clad with trees, so covered with bright red berries that hardly a leaf was to be seen. Soon the boat was almost within a stone's cast of the island, and it began to sail round and round until it was well under the bending branches. The scent of the berries was so sweet that it sharpened the prince's hunger, and he longed to pluck them; but, remembering what had happened to him on the enchanted island, he was afraid to touch them. But the boat kept on sailing round and round, and at last a great wind rose from the sea and shook the branches, and the bright, sweet berries fell into the boat until it was filled with them, and they fell upon the prince's hands, and he took up some to look at them, and as he looked the desire to eat them grew stronger, and he said to himself it would be no harm to taste one; but when he tasted it the flavour was so delicious he swallowed it, and, of course, at once he forgot all about Eileen, and the boat drifted away from him and left him standing in the water.

He climbed onto the island, and having eaten enough of the berries, he set out to see what might be before him, and it was not long until he heard a great noise, and a huge iron ball knocked down one of the trees in front of him, and before he knew where he was a hundred giants came running after it. When they saw the prince they turned towards him, and one of them caught him up in his hand and held him up that all might see him. The prince was nearly squeezed to death, and seeing this the giant put him on the ground again.

'Who are you, my little man?' asked the giant.

'I am a prince,' replied the prince.

'Oh, you are a prince, are you?' said the giant. 'And what are you good for?' said he.

The prince did not know, for nobody had asked him that question before.

'I know what he's good for,' said an old giantess, with one eye in her forehead and one in her chin. 'I know what he's good for. He's good to eat.'

When the giants heard this they laughed so loud that the prince was frightened almost to death.

'Why,' said one, 'he wouldn't make a mouthful.'

'Oh, leave him to me,' said the giantess, 'and I'll fatten him up; and when he is cooked and dressed he will be a nice dainty dish for the king.'

The giants, on this, gave the prince into the hands of the old giantess. She took him home with her to the kitchen, and fed him on sugar and spice and all things nice, so that he should be a sweet morsel for the king of the giants when he returned to the island. The poor prince would not eat anything at first, but the giantess held him over the fire until his feet were scorched, and then he said to himself it was better to eat than to be burnt alive.

Well, day after day passed, and the prince grew sadder and sadder, thinking that he would soon be cooked and dressed for the king; but sad as the prince was, he was not half as sad as the Princess Eileen in the giant's castle, watching and waiting for the prince to return and save her.

And the dwarfs had wound two balls, and were winding a third.

At last the prince heard from the old giantess that the king of the giants was to return on the following day, and she said to him:

'As this is the last night you have to live, tell me if you wish for anything, for if you do your wish will be granted.'

'I don't wish for anything,' said the prince, whose heart was dead within him.

'Well, I'll come back again,' said the giantess,

and she went away.

The prince sat down in a corner, thinking and thinking, until he heard close to his ear a sound like 'purr, purr!' He looked around, and there before him was the little white cat.

'I ought not to come to you,' said the cat; 'but, indeed, it is not for your sake I come. I come for the sake of Princess Eileen. Of course, you forgot all about her, and, of course, she is always thinking of you. It's always the way —

> Favoured lovers may forget,
> Slighted lovers never yet.

The prince blushed with shame when he heard the name of the princess.

' 'Tis you that ought to blush,' said the cat; 'but listen to me now, and remember, if you don't obey my directions this time you'll never see me again, and you'll never set your eyes on the Princess Eileen. When the old giantess comes back tell her you wish, when the morning comes, to go down to the sea to look at it for the last time. When you reach the sea you will know what to do. But I must go now, as I hear the giantess coming.' And the cat jumped out of the window and disappeared.

'Well,' said the giantess, when she came in, 'is there anything you wish?'

'Is it true I must die tomorrow?' asked the prince.

'It is.'

'Then,' said he, 'I should like to go down to the sea to look at it for the last time.'

'You may do that,' said the giantess, 'if you get up early.'

'I'll be up with the lark in the light of the morning,' said the prince.

'Very well,' said the giantess, and, saying 'good night,' she went away.

The prince thought the night would never pass, but at last it faded away before the grey light of the dawn, and he sped down to the sea. He threw out the third ball, and before long he saw the little boat coming towards him swifter than the wind. He threw himself into it the moment it touched the shore. Swifter than the wind it bore him out to sea, and before he had time to look behind him the island of the giantess was like a faint red speck in the distance. The day passed and the night fell, and the stars looked down, and the boat sailed on, and just as the sun rose above the sea it pushed its silver prow on the golden strand of an island greener than the leaves in summer. The prince jumped out, and went on and on until he entered a pleasant valley, at the head of which he saw a palace white as snow.

As he approached the central door it opened for him. On entering the hall he passed into several rooms without meeting with anyone; but, when he reached the principal apartment, he found himself in a circular room, in which were a thousand pillars, and every pillar was of marble, and on every pillar save one, which stood in the centre of the room, was a little white cat with black eyes. Ranged round the wall, from one door-jamb to the other, were three rows of precious jewels. The first was a row of brooches of gold and silver, with their pins fixed in the wall and their heads outwards; the second a row of torques of gold and silver; and the third a row of great swords, with hilts of gold and silver. And on many tables was food of all kinds, and drinking horns filled with foaming ale.[4]

While the prince was looking about him the cats kept on jumping from pillar to pillar; but seeing that none of them jumped on to the pillar in the centre of the room, he began to wonder why this was so, when, all of a sudden, and before he could guess how it came about, there right before him on the centre pillar was the little white cat.

'Don't you know me?' said he.

'I do,' said the prince.

'Ah, but you don't know who I am. This is the palace of the Little White Cat, and I am the King of the Cats. But you must be hungry, and the feast is spread.'

Well, when the feast was ended, the king of the cats called for the sword that would kill the giant Trencoss, and the hundred cakes for the hundred watch-dogs.

The cats brought the sword and the cakes and laid them before the king.

'Now,' said the king, 'take these; you have no time to lose. Tomorrow the dwarfs will wind the last ball, and tomorrow the giant will claim the princess for his bride. So you should go at once; but before you go take this from me to your little girl.'

And the king gave him a brooch lovelier than any on the palace walls.

The king and the prince, followed by the cats, went down to the strand, and when the prince stepped into the boat all the cats 'mewed' three times for good luck, and the prince waved his hat three times, and the little boat sped over the waters all through the night as brightly and as swiftly as a shooting star. In the first flush of morning it touched the strand. The prince jumped out and went on and on, up hill and down dale, until he came to the giant's castle. When the hounds saw him they barked furiously, and bounded towards him to tear him to pieces. The prince flung the cakes to them, and as each hound swallowed his cake he fell dead. The prince then struck his shield three times with the sword which he had brought from the palace of the little white cat.

When the giant heard the sound he cried out:

'Who comes to challenge me on my wedding-day?'

The dwarfs went out to see, and, returning, told him it was a prince who challenged him to battle.

The giant, foaming with rage, seized his heaviest iron club, and rushed out to the fight. The fight lasted the whole day, and when the sun went down the giant said:

'We have had enough of fighting for the day. We can begin at sunrise tomorrow.'

'Not so,' said the prince. 'Now or never; win or die.'

'Then take this,' cried the giant, as he aimed a blow with all his force at the prince's head; but the prince, darting forward like a flash of lightning drove his sword into the giant's heart, and, with a groan, he fell over the bodies of the poisoned hounds.

When the dwarfs saw the giant dead they began to cry and tear their hair. But the prince told them they had nothing to fear, and he bade them go and tell the Princess Eileen he wished to speak with her. But the princess had watched the battle from her window, and when she saw the giant fall she rushed out to greet the prince, and that very night he and she and all the dwarfs and harpers set out for the Palace of the Silver River, which they reached the next morning, and from that day to this there never has been a gayer wedding than the wedding of the Prince of the Silver River and the Princess Eileen; and though she had diamonds and pearls to spare, the only jewel she wore on her wedding-day was the brooch which the prince had brought her from the Palace of the Little White Cat in the far-off seas.

THE GOLDEN SPEARS

Once upon a time there lived in a little house under a hill a little old woman and her two children, whose names were Connla and Nora. Right in front of the door of the little house lay a pleasant meadow, and beyond the meadow rose up to the skies a mountain whose top was sharp-pointed like a spear. For more than half-way up it was clad with heather, and when the heather was in bloom it looked like a purple robe falling from the shoulders of the mountain down to its feet. Above the heather it was bare and grey, but when the sun was sinking in the sea, its last rays rested on the bare mountain top and made it gleam like a spear of gold, and so the children always called it the 'Golden Spear.'

In summer days they gambolled in the meadow, plucking the sweet wild grasses — and often and often they clambered up the mountain side, knee deep in the heather, searching for frechans and wild honey, and sometimes they found a bird's nest   but they only peeped into it, they never touched the eggs or allowed their breath to fall upon them, for next to their little mother they loved the mountain, and next to the mountain they loved the wild birds who made the spring and summer weather musical with their songs.

Sometimes the soft white mist would steal through the glen, and creeping up the mountain

55

would cover it with a veil so dense that the children could not see it, and then they would say to each other: 'Our mountain is gone away from us.' But when the mist would lift and float off into the skies, the children would clap their hands, and say: 'Oh, there's our mountain back again.'

In the long nights of winter they babbled of the spring and summertime to come, when the birds would once more sing for them, and never a day passed that they didn't fling crumbs outside their door, and on the borders of the wood that stretched away towards the glen.

When the spring days came they awoke with the first light of the morning, and they knew the very minute when the lark would begin to sing, and when the thrush and the blackbird would pour out their liquid notes, and when the robin would make the soft, green, tender leaves tremulous at his song.

It chanced one day that when they were resting in the noontide heat, under the perfumed shade of a hawthorn in bloom, they saw on the edge of the meadow, spread out before them, a speckled thrush cowering in the grass.

'Oh, Connla! Connla! Look at the thrush — and, look, look up in the sky, there is a hawk!' cried Nora.

Connla looked up, and he saw the hawk with quivering wings, and he knew that in a second it would pounce down on the frightened thrush. He jumped to his feet, fixed a stone in his sling, and before the whirr of the stone shooting through the air was silent, the stricken hawk tumbled headlong in the grass.

The thrush, shaking its wings, rose joyously in the air, and perching upon an elm-tree in sight of

the children, he sang a song so sweet that they left
the hawthorn shade and walked along together
until they stood under the branches of the elm;
and they listened and listened to the thrush's song,
and at last Nora said:

'Oh, Connla! did you ever hear a song so sweet
as this?'

'No,' said Connla, 'and I do believe sweeter
music was never heard before.'

'Ah,' said the thrush, 'that's because you never
heard the nine little pipers playing. And now,
Connla and Nora, you saved my life today.'

'It was Nora saved it,' said Connla, 'for she pointed you out to me, and also pointed out the hawk
which was about to pounce on you.'

'It was Connla saved you,' said Nora, 'for he
slew the hawk with his sling.'

'I owe my life to both of you,' said the thrush.
'You like my song, and you say you have never
heard anything so sweet; but wait till you hear the
nine little pipers playing.'

'And when shall we hear them?' said the children.

'Well,' said the thrush, 'sit outside your door tomorrow evening, and wait and watch until the
shadows have crept up the heather, and then, when
the mountain top is gleaming like a golden spear,
look at the line where the shadow on the heather
meets the sunshine, and you shall see what you
shall see.'

And having said this, the thrush sang another
song sweeter than the first, and then saying 'good-
bye,' he flew away into the woods.

The children went home, and all night long they
were dreaming of the thrush and the nine little
pipers; and when the birds sang in the morning,

they got up and went out into the meadow to watch the mountain.

The sun was shining in a cloudless sky, and no shadows lay on the mountain, and all day long they watched and waited, and at last, when the birds were singing their farewell song to the evening star, the children saw the shadows marching from the glen, trooping up the mountain side and dimming the purple of the heather.

And when the mountain top gleamed like a golden spear, they fixed their eyes on the line between the shadow and the sunshine.

'Now,' said Connla, 'the time has come.'

'Oh, look! look!' said Nora, and as she spoke, just above the line of shadow a door opened out, and through its portals came a little piper dressed in green and gold. He stepped down, followed by another and another, until they were nine in all, and then the door slung back again. Down through the heather marched the pipers in single file, and all the time they played a music so sweet that the birds, who had gone to sleep in their nests, came out upon the branches to listen to them, and then they crossed the meadow, and they went on and on until they disappeared in the leafy woods.

While they were passing the children were spellbound, and couldn't speak, but when the music had died away in the woods, they said:

'The thrush is right, that is the sweetest music that was ever heard in all the world.'

And when the children went to bed that night the fairy music came to them in their dreams. But when the morning broke, and they looked out upon their mountain and could see no trace of the door above the heather, they asked each other whether they had really seen the little pipers, or only dreamt of them.

That day they went out into the woods, and they sat beside a stream that pattered along beneath the trees, and through the leaves tossing in the breeze the sun flashed down upon the streamlet, and shadow and sunshine danced upon it. As the children watched the water sparkling where the sunlight fell, Nora said:

'Oh, Connla, did you ever see anything so bright and clear and glancing as that?'

'No,' said Connla, 'I never did.'

'That's because you never saw the crystal hall of the fairy of the mountains,' said a voice above the heads of the children.

And when they looked up, who should they see perched on a branch but the thrush.

'And where is the crystal hall of the fairy?' said Connla.

'Oh, it is where it always was, and where it always will be,' said the thrush. 'And you can see it if you like.'

'We would like to see it,' said the children.

'Well, then,' said the thrush, 'if you would, all you have to do is to follow the nine little pipers when they come down through the heather, and cross the meadow tomorrow evening.'

And the thrush having said this, flew away.

Connla and Nora went home, and that night they fell asleep talking of the thrush and the fairy and the crystal hall.

All the next day they counted the minutes, until they saw the shadows thronging from the glen and scaling the mountain side. And, at last, they saw the door springing open, and the nine little pipers marching down.

They waited until the pipers had crossed the meadow and were about to enter the wood. And then they followed them, the pipers marching on before them and playing all the time. It was not long until they had passed through the wood, and then, what should the children see rising up before them but another mountain, smaller than their own, but, like their own, clad more than half-way up with purple heather, and whose top was bare and sharp-pointed, and gleaming like a golden spear.

Up through the heather climbed the pipers, up through the heather the children clambered after them, and the moment the pipers passed the heather a door opened and they marched in, the children following, and the door closed behind them.

Connla and Nora were so dazzled by the light that hit their eyes, when they had crossed the threshold, that they had to shade them with their hands; but, after a moment or two, they became able to bear the splendour, and when they looked around they saw that they were in a noble hall, whose crystal roof was supported by two rows of crystal pillars rising from a crystal floor; and the walls were of crystal, and along the walls were crystal couches, with coverings and cushions of sapphire silk with silver tassels.

Over the crystal floor the little pipers marched; over the crystal floor the children followed, and when a door at the end of the hall was opened to let the pipers pass, a crowd of colours came rushing in, and floor, and ceiling, and stately pillars, and glancing couches, and shining walls, were stained with a thousand dazzling hues.

Out through the door the pipers marched; out through the door the children followed, and when they crossed the threshold they were treading on clouds of amber, of purple, and of gold.

'Oh, Connla,' said Nora, 'we have walked into the sunset!'

And around and about them everywhere were soft, fleecy clouds, and over their heads was the glowing sky, and the stars were shining through it, as a lady's eyes shine through a veil of gossamer. And the sky and stars seemed so near that Connla thought he could almost touch them with his hand.

When they had gone some distance, the pipers disappeared, and when Connla and Nora came up to the spot where they had seen the last of them, they found themselves at the head of a ladder, all the steps of which were formed of purple and amber clouds that descended to what appeared to be a vast and shining plain, streaked with purple and gold. In the spaces between the streaks of gold and purple they saw soft, milk-white stars. And the children thought that the great plain, so far below them, also belonged to cloudland.

They could not see the little pipers, but up the steps was borne by the cool, sweet air the fairy music; and lured on by it step by step they travelled down the fleecy stairway. When they were a little more than half way down there came mingled with the music a sound almost as sweet — the sound of waters toying in the still air with pebbles on a shelving beach, and with the sound came the odorous brine of the ocean. And then the children knew that what they thought was a plain in the realms of cloudland was the sleeping sea unstirred by wind or tide, dreaming of the purple clouds and stars of the sunset sky above it.

When Connla and Nora reached the strand they saw the nine little pipers marching out towards the sea, and they wondered where they were going to. And they could hardly believe their eyes when they saw them stepping out upon the level ocean as if they were walking upon the land; and away the nine little pipers marched, treading the golden line cast upon the waters by the setting sun. And as the music became fainter and fainter as the pipers passed into the glowing distance, the children began to wonder what was to become of themselves. Just at that very moment they saw coming towards them from the sinking sun a little white horse, with flowing mane and tail and golden hoofs. On the horse's back was a little man dressed in shining green silk. When the horse galloped on to the strand the little man doffed his hat, and said to the children:

'Would you like to follow the nine little pipers?' The children said, 'yes.'

'Well, then,' said the little man, 'come up here behind me; you, Nora, first, and Connla after.'

Connla helped up Nora, and then climbed on to the little steed himself; and as soon as they were properly seated the little man said 'swish', and away went the steed, galloping over the sea without wetting hair or hoof. But fast as he galloped the nine little pipers were always ahead of him, although they seemed to be going only at a walking pace. When at last he came up rather close to the hindmost of them the nine little pipers disappeared, but the children heard the music playing beneath the waters. The white steed pulled up suddenly, and wouldn't move a step further.

'Now,' said the little man to the children, 'clasp me tight, Nora, and do you, Connla, cling on to Nora, and both of you shut your eyes.'

The children did as they were bidden, and the little man cried:

'Swish! swash!'

And the steed went down and down until at last his feet struck the bottom.

'Now open your eyes,' said the little man.

And when the children did so they saw beneath the horse's feet a golden strand, and above their heads the sea like a transparent cloud between them and the sky. And once more they heard the fairy music, and marching on the strand before them were the nine little pipers.

'You must get off now,' said the little man, 'I can go no farther with you.'

The children scrambled down, and the little man cried, 'swish,' and himself and the steed shot up through the sea, and they saw him no more. Then they set out after the nine little pipers, and it wasn't long until they saw rising up from the golden strand and pushing their heads up into the sea above, a mass of dark grey rocks. And as they were gazing at them they saw the rocks opening, and the nine little pipers disappearing through them.

The children hurried on, and when they came up close to the rocks they saw sitting on a flat and polished stone a mermaid combing her golden hair, and singing a strange sweet song that brought the tears to their eyes, and by the mermaid's side was a little sleek brown otter.

When the mermaid saw them she flung her golden tresses back over her snow-white shoulders, and she beckoned the children to her. Her large eyes were full of sadness. but there was a look so tender upon her face that the children moved towards her without any fear.

'Come to me, little one,' she said to Nora, 'come and kiss me,' and in a second her arms were around the child. The mermaid kissed her again and again, as the tears rushed to her eyes, she said:

'Oh, Nora, avourneen, your breath is as sweet as the wild rose that blooms in the green fields of Erin, and happy are you, my children, who have come so lately from the pleasant land. Oh, Connla! Connla! I get the scent of the dew of the Irish grasses and of the purple heather from your feet. And you both can soon return to Erin of the Streams, but I shall not see it till three hundred years have passed away, for I am Liban the Mermaid, daughter of a line of kings. But I may not keep you here. The Fairy Queen is waiting for you in her snow-white palace and her fragrant bowers. And now kiss me once more, Nora, and kiss me, Connla. May luck and joy go with you, and all gentleness be upon you both.'[5]

Then the children said goodbye to the mermaid, and the rocks opened for them and they passed through, and soon they found themselves in a meadow starred with flowers, and through the meadow sped a sunlit stream. They followed the stream until it led them into a garden of roses, and beyond the garden, standing on a gentle hill, was a palace white as snow. Before the palace was a crowd of fairy maidens pelting each other with rose-leaves. But when they saw the children they gave over their play, and came trooping towards them.

'Our queen is waiting for you,' they said; and then they led the children to the palace door. The

64

children entered, and after passing through a long corridor they found themselves in a crystal hall so like the one they had seen in the mountain of the golden spear that they thought it was the same. But on all the crystal couches fairies, dressed in silken robes of many colours, were sitting, and at the end of the hall, on a crystal throne, was seated the fairy queen, looking lovelier than the evening star. The queen descended from her throne to meet the children, and taking them by the hands, she led them up the shining steps. Then sitting down, she made them sit beside her, Connla on her right hand and Nora on her left.

Then she ordered the nine little pipers to come before her, and she said to them:

'So far you have done your duty faithfully, and now play one more sweet air and your task is done.'

And the little pipers played, and from the couches at the first sound of the music all the fairies rose, and forming partners, they danced over the crystal floor as lightly as the young leaves dancing in the wind.

Listening to the fairy music, and watching the wavy motion of the dancing fairies, the children fell asleep. When they awoke next morning and rose from their silken beds they were no longer children. Nora was a graceful and stately maiden, and Connla a handsome and gallant youth. They looked at each other for a moment in surprise, and then Connla said:

'Oh, Nora, how tall and beautiful you are!'

'Oh, not so tall and handsome as you are, Connla,' said Nora, as she flung her white arms round his neck and kissed her brother's lips.

Then they drew back to get a better look of

each other, and who should step between them but the fairy queen.

'Oh, Nora, Nora,' said she, 'I am not as high as your knee, and as for you, Connla, you look as straight and as tall as one of the round towers of Erin.'

'And how did we grow so tall in one night?' said Connla.

'In one night!' said the fairy queen. 'One night, indeed! Why, you have been fast asleep, the two of you, for the last seven years!'

And where was the little mother all that time?' said Connla and Nora together.

'Oh, the little mother was all right. She knew where you were; but she is expecting you today, and so you must go off to see her, although I would like to keep you — if I had my way — all to myself here in the fairyland under the sea. And you will see her today; but before you go here is a necklace for you, Nora; it is formed out of the drops of the ocean spray, sparkling in the sunshine. They were caught by my fairy nymph, for you, as they skimmed the sunlit billows under the shape of sea-birds, and no queen or princess in the world can match their lustre with the diamonds won with toil from the caves of earth. As for you, Connla, see here's a helmet of shining gold fit for a king of Erin — and a king of Erin you will be yet; and here's a spear that will pierce any shield, and here's a shield that no spear can pierce and no sword can cleave as long as you fasten your warrior cloak with this brooch of gold.'

And as she spoke she flung round Connla's shoulders a flowing mantle of yellow silk, and pinned it at his neck with a red gold brooch.

66

'And now, my children, you must go away from me. You, Nora, will be a warrior's bride in Erin of the Streams. And you, Connla, will be king yet over the loveliest province in all the land of Erin; but you will have to fight for your crown, and days of battle are before you. They will not come for a long time after you have left the fairyland under the sea, and until they come lay aside your helmet, shield, and spear, and warrior's cloak and golden brooch. But when the time comes when you will be called to battle, enter not upon it without the golden brooch I give you fastened in your cloak, for if you do harm will come to you. Now, kiss me, children; your little mother is waiting for you at the foot of the golden spear, but do not forget to say goodbye to Liban the Mermaid, exiled from the land she loves, and pining in sadness beneath the sea.'

Connla and Nora kissed the fairy queen, and Connla, wearing his golden helmet and silken cloak, and carrying his shield and spear, led Nora with him. They passed from the palace through the garden of roses, through the flowery meadow, through the dark grey rocks, until they reached the golden strand; and there, sitting and singing the strange, sweet song, was Liban the Mermaid.

'And so you are going up to Erin,' she said, 'up through the covering waters. Kiss me, children, once again; and when you are in Erin of the Streams, sometimes think of the exile from Erin beneath the sea.'

And the children kissed the mermaid, and with sad hearts, bidding her goodbye, they walked along the golden strand. When they had gone what seemed to them a long way, they began to feel weary;

67

and just then they saw coming towards them a little man in a red jacket leading a coal-black steed.

When they met the little man, he said: 'Connla, put Nora up on this steed; then jump up before her.'

Connla did as he was told, and when both of them were mounted —

'Now, Connla,' said the little man, 'catch the bridle in your hands, and you, Nora, clasp Connla round the waist, and close your eyes.'

They did as they were bidden, and then the little man said, 'Swash, swish!' and the steed shot up from the strand like a lark from the grass, and pierced the covering sea, and went bounding on over the level waters; and when his hoofs struck the hard ground, Connla and Nora opened their eyes, and they saw that they were galloping towards a shady wood.

On went the steed, and soon he was galloping beneath the branches that almost touched Connla's head. And on they went until they had passed through the wood, and then they saw rising up before them the 'Golden Spear'.

'Oh, Connla,' said Nora, 'we are at home at last.'

'Yes,' said Connla, 'but where is the little house under the hill?'

And no little house was there; but in its stead was standing a lime-white mansion.

'What can this mean?' said Nora.

But before Connla could reply, the steed had galloped up to the door of the mansion, and, in the twinkling of an eye, Connla and Nora were standing on the ground outside the door, and the steed had vanished.

Before they could recover from their surprise the little mother came rushing out to them, and flung her arms around their necks, and kissed them both again and again.

'Oh, children! children! You are welcome home to me; for though I knew it was all for the best, my heart was lonely without you.'

And Connla and Nora caught up the little mother in their arms, and they carried her into the hall and set her down on the floor.

'Oh, Nora!' said the little mother, 'you are a head over me; and as for you, Connla, you look almost as tall as one of the round towers of Erin.'

'That's what the fairy queen said, mother,' said Nora.

'Blessings on the fairy queen,' said the little mother. 'Turn round, Connla, till I look at you.'

Connla turned round, and the little mother said:

'Oh, Connla, with your golden helmet and your spear, and your glancing shield, and your silken cloak, you look like a king. But take them off, my boy, beautiful as they are. Your little mother would like to see you, her own brave boy, without any fairy finery.'

And Connla laid aside his spear and shield, and took off his golden helmet and his silken cloak. Then he caught the little mother and kissed her, and lifted her up until she was as high as his head. And said he:

'Don't you know, little mother, I'd rather have you than all the world.'

And that night, when they were sitting down by the fire together, you may be sure that in the whole world no people were half as happy as Nora, Connla, and the little mother.

THE FAIRY TREE OF DOOROS[6]

Once upon a time the fairies of the west, going home from a hurling-match with the fairies of the lakes, rested in Dooros Wood for three days and three nights. They spent the days feasting and the nights dancing in the light of the moon, and they danced so hard that they wore the shoes off their feet, and for a whole week after the leprechauns, the fairies' shoemakers, were working night and day making new ones, and the rip, rap, tap, tap of their little hammers were heard in all the hedgerows.

The food on which the fairies feasted were little red berries, and were so like those that grow on the rowan tree that if you only looked at them you might mistake one for the other; but the fairy berries grow only in fairyland, and are sweeter than any fruit that grows here in this world, and if an old man, bent and grey, ate one of them, he became young and active and strong again; and if an old woman, withered and wrinkled, ate one of them, she became young and bright and fair; and if a little maiden who was not handsome ate of them, she became lovelier than the flower of beauty.

The fairies guarded the berries as carefully as a miser guards his gold, and whenever they were about to leave fairyland they had to promise in the presence of the king and queen that they would not give a single berry to mortal man, nor allow one to fall upon the earth; for if a single berry fell upon the earth a slender tree of many branches, bearing clusters of berries, would at once spring up, and mortal men might eat of them.

But it chanced that this time they were in Dooros Wood they kept up the feasting and dancing so long, and were so full of joy because of their victory over the lake fairies, that one little, weeny fairy, not much bigger than my finger, lost his head, and dropped a berry in the wood.

When the feast was ended the fairies went back to fairyland, and were at home for more than a week before they knew of the little fellow's fault, and this is how they came to know of it.

A great wedding was about to come off, and the queen of the fairies sent six of her pages to Dooros Wood to catch fifty butterflies with golden spots on their purple wings, and fifty white without speck or spot, and fifty golden, yellow as the cow-slip, to make a dress for herself, and a hundred white, without speck or spot, to make dresses for the bride and bridesmaids.

When the pages came near the wood they heard the most wonderful music, and the sky above them became quite dark, as if a cloud had shut out the sun. They looked up, and saw that the cloud was formed of bees, who in a great swarm were flying towards the wood and humming as they flew. Seeing this they were sore afraid until they saw the bees settling on a single tree, and on looking closely at the tree they saw it was covered with fairy berries.

The bees took no notice of the fairies, and so they were no longer afraid, and they hunted the butterflies until they had captured the full number of various colours. Then they returned to fairyland,

and they told the queen about the bees and the berries, and the queen told the king.

The king was very angry, and he sent his heralds to the four corners of fairyland to summon all his subjects to his presence that he might find out without delay who was the culprit.

They all came except the little weeny fellow who dropped the berry, and of course everyone said that it was fear that kept him away, and that he must be guilty.

The heralds were at once sent in search of him, and after a while they found him hiding in a cluster of ferns, and brought him before the king.

The poor little fellow was so frightened that at first he could scarcely speak a word, but after a time he told how he never missed the berry until he had returned to fairyland, and that he was afraid to say anything to anyone about it.

The king, who would hear of no excuse, sentenced the little culprit to be banished into the land of giants beyond the mountains, to stay there forever and a day unless he could find a giant willing to go to Dooros Wood and guard the fairy tree. When the king had pronounced sentence everyone was very sorry, because the little fellow was a favourite with them all. No fairy harper upon his harp, or piper upon his pipe, or fiddler upon his fiddle, could play half so sweetly as he could play on an ivy leaf; and when they remembered all the pleasant moon-lit nights on which they had danced to his music, and thought that they should never hear or dance to it any more, their little hearts were filled with sorrow. The queen was as sad as any of her subjects, but the king's word should be obeyed.

When the time came for the little fellow to set

out into exile the queen sent her head page to him with a handful of berries. These the queen said he was to offer to the giants, and say at the same time that the giant who was willing to guard the tree could feast on berries just as sweet from morn till night.

As the little fellow went on his way nearly all the fairies followed him to the borders of the land, and when they saw him go up the mountain towards the land of the giants, they all took off their little red caps and waved them until he was out of sight.

On he went walking all day and night, and when the sun rose on the morrow he was on the top of the mountain, and he could see the land of the giants in the valley stretched far below him. Before beginning his descent he turned round for a last glimpse of fairyland; but he could see nothing, for a thick, dark cloud shut it out from view. He was very sad, and tired, and footsore, and as he struggled down the rough mountain side, he could not help thinking of the soft, green woods and mossy pathways of the pleasant land he had left behind him.

When he awoke the ground was trembling, and a noise that sounded like thunder fell on his ears. He looked up and saw coming towards him a terrible giant, with one eye that burned like a live coal in the middle of his forehead, his mouth stretched from ear to ear, his teeth were long and crooked, the skin of his face was as black as night, and his arms and chest were all covered with black, shaggy hair; round his body was an iron band, and hanging from this by a chain was a great club with iron spikes. With one blow of this club he could break a rock into splinters, and fire could not burn him, and water could not drown him, and weapons could not wound him, and there was no way to kill him but by giving him three blows of his own club. And he was so bad-tempered that the other giants called him Sharvan the Surly. When the giant spied the red cap of the little fairy he gave the shout that sounded like thunder. The poor fairy was shaking from head to foot.

'What brought you here?' said the giant.

'Please, Mr Giant,' said the fairy, 'the king of the fairies banished me here, and here I must stay for ever and a day, unless you come and guard the fairy tree in Dooros Wood.'

'Unless what?' roared the giant, and he gave the fairy a touch of his foot that sent the little fellow rolling down head over heels.

The poor fairy lay as if he were dead, and then the giant, feeling sorry for what he had done, took him up gently between his finger and thumb.

'Don't be frightened, little man,' said he, 'and now, tell me all about the tree.'

'It is the tree of the fairy berry that grows in the Wood of Dooros,' said the fairy, 'and I have some of the berries with me.'

'Oh, you have, have you?' said the giant. 'Let me see them.'

The fairy took three berries from the pocket of his little green coat, and gave them to the giant.

The giant looked at them for a second. He then swallowed the three together, and when he had done so, he felt so happy that he began to shout and dance for joy.

'More, you little thief!' said he. 'More, you little what's your name?' said the giant.

74

'Pinkeen, please, Mr Giant,' said the fairy, as he gave up all the berries.

The giant shouted louder than before, and his shouts were heard by all the other giants, who came running towards him.

When Sharvan saw them coming, he caught up Pinkeen, and put him in his pocket, that they shouldn't see him.

'What were you shouting for?' said the giants.

'Because,' said Sharvan, 'that rock there fell down on my big toe.'

'You did not shout like a man that was hurt,' said they.

'What is it to you what way I shouted?' said he.

'You might give a civil answer to a civil question,' said they; 'but sure you were always Sharvan the Surly,' and they went away.

When the giants were out of sight, Sharvan took Pinkeen out of his wallet.

'Some more berries, you little thief — I mean little Pinkeen,' said he.

'I have not any more,' said Pinkeen; 'but if you will guard the tree in Dooros Wood you can feast on them from morn till night.'

'I'll guard every tree in the wood, if I may do that,' said the giant.

'You'll have to guard only one,' said Pinkeen.

'How am I to get to it?' said Sharvan.

'You must first come with me towards fairyland,' said the fairy.

'Very well,' said Sharvan; 'let us go.' And he took up the fairy and put him into his wallet, and before very long they were on top of the mountain. Then the giant looked around towards the giant's land; but a black cloud shut it out from view, while

75

the sun was shining on the valley that lay before him, and he could see away in the distance the green woods and shining waters of fairyland.

It was not long until he reached its borders, but when he tried to cross them his feet stuck to the ground and he could not move a step. Sharvan gave three loud shouts that were heard all over fairyland, and made the trees in the woods tremble, as if the wind of a storm was sweeping over them.

'Oh, please, Mr Giant, let me out,' said Pinkeen. Sharvan took out the little fellow, who, as soon as he saw he was on the borders of fairyland ran as fast as his legs could carry him, and before he had gone very far he met all the little fairies who, hearing the shouts of the giant, came trooping out from the ferns to see what was the matter. Pinkeen told them it was the giant who was to guard the tree, shouting because he was stuck fast on the borders, and they need have no fear of him. The fairies were so delighted to have Pinkeen back again, that they took him up on their shoulders and carried him to the king's palace, and all the harpers and pipers and fiddlers marched before him playing the most jocund music that was ever heard. The king and queen were on the lawn in front of the palace when the gay procession came up and halted before them. The queen's eyes glistened with pleasure when she saw the little favourite, and the king was also glad at heart, but he looked very grave as he said:

'Why have you returned, sirrah?'

Then Pinkeen told his majesty that he had brought with him a giant who was willing to guard the fairy tree.

'And who is he and where is he?' asked the king.

'The other giants called him Sharvan the Surly,' said Pinkeen, 'and he is stuck fast outside the borders of fairyland.'

'It is well,' said the king, 'you are pardoned.'

When the fairies heard this they tossed their little red caps in the air, and cheered so loudly that a bee who was clinging to a rose-bud fell senseless to the ground.

Then the king ordered one of his pages to take a handful of berries, and to go to Sharvan and show him the way to Dooros Wood. The page, taking the berries with him, went off to Sharvan, whose roaring nearly frightened the poor little fellow to death. But as soon as the giant tasted the berries he got into good humour, and he asked the page if he could remove the spell of enchantment from him.

'I can,' said the page, 'and I will if you promise me that you will not try to cross the borders of fairyland.'

'I promise that, with all my heart,' said the giant. 'But hurry on, my little man, for there are pins and needles in my legs.'

The page plucked a cowslip, and picking out the five little crimson spots in the cup of it, he flung one to the north, and one to the south, and one to the east, and one to the west, and one up into the sky, and the spell was broken, and the giant's limbs were free. Then Sharvan and the fairy page set off for Dooros Wood, and it was not long until they came within view of the fairy tree. When Sharvan saw the berries glistening in the sun, he gave a shout so loud and strong that the wind of it blew the little fairy back to fairyland. But he had to return to the wood to tell the giant that he was to stay all day at the foot of the tree ready to do battle with anyone who might come to steal the berries, and that during the night he was to sleep amongst the branches.

'All right,' said the giant, who could scarcely speak, as his mouth was full of berries.

Well, the fame of the fairy-tree spread far and wide, and every day some adventurer came to try if he could carry away some of the berries; but the giant, true to his word, was always on the watch, and not a single day passed on which he did not fight and slay a daring champion, and the giant never received a wound, for fire could not burn him, nor water drown him, nor weapon wound him.

Now, at this time, when Sharvan was keeping watch and ward over the tree, a cruel king was reigning over the lands that looked towards the rising sun. He had slain the rightful king by foul means, and his subjects, loving their murdered sovereign, hated the usurper; but much as they hated him they feared him more, for he was brave and masterful, and he was armed with a helmet and shield which no weapon made by mortal hands could pierce, and he carried always with him two javelins that never missed their mark, and were so fatal that they were called 'the shafts of death.' The murdered king had two children — a boy, whose name was Niall, and a girl, who was called Rosaleen — that is, little Rose; but no rose that ever bloomed was half as sweet or fresh or fair as she. Cruel as the tyrant king was, he was afraid of the people to kill the children. He sent the boy adrift on the sea in an open boat, hoping the waves would swallow it; and he got an old witch to cast the spell of deformity over Rosaleen, and under the spell her beauty faded, until at last she became so ugly and wasted that scarcely anyone would speak to her. And, shunned by everyone, she spent her days in the out-houses with the cattle, and every night she cried herself to sleep.

One day, when she was very lonely, a little robin came to pick the crumbs that had fallen about her feet. He appeared so tame that she offered him the bread from her hand, and when he took it she cried with joy at finding that there was one living thing that did not shun her. After this the robin came every day, and he sang so sweetly for her that she almost forgot her loneliness and misery. But once while the robin was with her the tyrant king's daughter, who was very beautiful, passed with her maids of honour, and, seeing Rosaleen, the princess said:

'Oh, there is that horrid ugly thing.'

The maids laughed and giggled, and said they had never seen such a fright.

Poor Rosaleen felt as if her heart would break, and when the princess and her maids were out of sight she almost cried her eyes out. When the robin saw her crying he perched on her shoulder and rubbed his little head against her neck and chirruped softly in her ear, and Rosaleen was comforted, for she felt she had at least one friend in the world, although it was only a little robin. But the robin could do more for her than she could dream of. He heard the remark made by the princess, and he saw Rosaleen's tears, and he knew now why she was shunned by everybody, and why she was so unhappy. And that very evening he flew off to Dooros Wood, and called on a cousin of his and told him all about Rosaleen.

'And you want some of the fairy berries, I

suppose,' said his cousin, Robin of the Wood.

'I do,' said Rosaleen's little friend.

'Ah,' said Robin of the Wood, 'times have changed since you were here last. The tree is guarded now all the day long by a surly giant. He sleeps in the branches during the night, and he breathes upon them and around them every morning, and his breath is poison to bird and bee. There is only one chance open, and if you try that it may cost you your life.'

'Then tell me what it is, for I would give a hundred lives for Rosaleen,' said her own little robin.

'Well,' said Robin of the Wood, 'every day a champion comes to battle with the giant, and the giant, before he begins the fight, puts a branch of berries in the iron belt that's around his waist, so that when he feels tired or thirsty he can refresh himself, and there is just a bare chance, while he is fighting, of picking one of the berries from the branch; but if his breath fall on you it is certain death.'

'I will take the chance,' said Rosaleen's robin.

'Very well,' said the other. And the two birds flew through the wood until they came within sight of the fairy tree. The giant was lying stretched at the foot of it, eating the berries; but it was not long until a warrior came, who challenged him to battle. The giant jumped up, and plucking a branch from the tree stuck it in his belt, and swinging his iron club above his head strode towards the warrior, and the fight began. The robin perched on a tree behind the giant, and watched and waited for his chance; but it was a long time coming, for the berries were in front of the giant's belt. At last the giant, with one great blow, struck the warrior down, but as he did so he stumbled and fell upon him, and before he had time to recover himself the little robin darted towards him like a flash and picked off one of the berries, and then, as fast as wings could carry him, he flew towards home, and on his way he passed over a troop of warriors on snow-white steeds. All the horsemen except one wore silver helmets and shining mantles of green silk, fastened by brooches of red gold, but the chief, who rode at the head of the troop, wore a golden helmet, and his mantle was of yellow silk, and he looked by far the noblest of them all. When the robin had left the horsemen far behind him he spied Rosaleen sitting outside the palace gates bemoaning her fate. The robin perched upon her shoulder, and almost before she knew he was there he put the berry between her lips, and the taste was so delicious that Rosaleen ate it at once, and that very moment the witch's withering spell passed away from her, and she became as lovely as the flower of beauty. Just then the warriors on the snow-white steeds came up, and the chief with the mantle of yellow silk and the golden helmet leaped from his horse, and bending his knee before her, said:

'Fairest of all fair maidens, you are surely the daughter of the king of these realms, even though you are without the palace gates, unattended, and wear not royal robes. I am the Prince of the Sunny Valleys.'

'Daughter of a king I am,' said Rosaleen, 'but not of the king who rules these realms.'

And saying this she fled, leaving the prince wondering who she could be. The prince then ordered his trumpeters to give notice of his presence outside the palace, and in a few moments the king and all his nobles came out to greet the prince and his warriors, and give them welcome. That night a great feast was spread in the banquet-hall, and the Prince of the Sunny Valleys sat by the king, and beside the prince sat the king's beautiful daughter, and then in due order sat the nobles of the court and the warriors who had come with the prince, and on the wall behind each noble and warrior his shield and helmet were suspended, flashing radiance through the room. During the feast the prince spoke most graciously to the lovely lady at his side, but all the time he was thinking of the unknown beauty he had met outside the palace gates, and his heart longed for another glimpse of her. When the feast was ended, and the jewelled drinking-cups had gone merrily around the table, the bards sang, to the accompaniment of harps, the *Courtship of the Lady Eimer*, and as they pictured her radiant beauty outshining that of all her maidens, the prince thought that fair as Lady Eimer was there was one still fairer.

When the feast was ended the king asked the prince what brought him into his realms.

'I come,' said the prince, 'to look for a bride, for it was foretold to me in my own country that here only I should find the lady who is destined to share my throne, and fame reported that in your kingdom are to be found the loveliest maidens in all the world, and I can well believe that,' added the price, 'after what I have seen today.'

When the king's daughter heard this she hung down her head and blushed like a rose, for, of course, she thought the prince was alluding only to herself, as she did not know that he had seen Rosaleen, and she had not heard of the restoration of her beauty.

Before another word could be spoken a great noise and the clang of arms were heard outside the palace. The king and his guests started from their seats and drew their swords, and the bards raised the song of battle; but their voices were stilled and their harps silenced when they saw at the threshold of the banquet-hall a battle champion, in whose face they recognised the features of their murdered king.

' 'Tis Niall come back to claim his father's throne,' said the chief bard. 'Long live Niall!'

'Long live Niall!' answered all the others.

The king, white with rage and amazement, turned to the chiefs and nobles of his court, and cried out:

'Is there none loyal enough to drive that intruder from the banquet-hall?'

But no one stirred, and no answer was given. Then the king rushed forward alone, but before he could reach the spot where Niall was standing he was seized by a dozen chiefs and at once disarmed.

During this scene the king's daughter had fled frightened; but Rosaleen, attracted by the noise, and hearing her brother's name and the cheers which greeted it, had entered the banquet-hall unperceived by anyone. But when her presence was discovered every eye was dazzled with her beauty. Niall looked at her for a second, wondering if the radiant maiden before him could be the little sister he had been separated from for so many years. In another second she was clasped in his arms.

Then the feast was spread again, and Niall told the story of his adventures; and when the Prince of the Sunny Valleys asked for the hand of Rosaleen, Niall told his lovely sister to speak for herself. With downcast eyes and smiling lips she said, 'yes,' and that very day was the gayest and brightest wedding that ever took place, and Rosaleen became the prince's bride.

In her happiness she did not forget the little robin, who was her friend in sorrow. She took him home with her to Sunny Valleys, and every day she fed him with her own hands, and every day he sang for her the sweetest songs that were ever heard in lady's bower.

THE ENCHANTED CAVE

A long, long time ago, Prince Cuglas,[7] master of the hounds to the high King of Erin, set out from Tara to the chase. As he was leaving the palace the light mists were drifting away from the hill-tops, and the rays of the morning sun were falling aslant on the *grinan* or sunny bower of the Princess Ailinn. Glancing towards it the prince doffed his plumed and jewelled hunting-cap, and the princess answered his salute by a wave of her little hand, that was as white as a wild rose in the hedges in June, and leaning from her bower, she watched the huntsman until his tossing plumes were hidden by the green waving branches of the woods.

The Princess Ailinn was over head and ears in love with Cuglas, and Cuglas was over head and ears in love with the Princess Ailinn, and he believed that never was summer morning half as bright, or as sweet, or as fair as she. The glimpse which he had just caught of her filled his heart with delight, and almost put all thought of hunting out of his head, when suddenly the tuneful cries of the hounds, answered by a hundred echoes from the groves broke upon his ear.

The dogs had started a dappled deer that bounded away through the forest. The prince, spurring his gallant steed, pushed on in eager pursuit.

On through the forest sped the deer, through soft, green, secret ways and flowery dells, then out from the forest, up heathery hills, and over long stretches of moorland, and across brown rushing streams, sometimes in view of the hounds, sometimes lost to sight, but always ahead of them.

All day long the chase continued, and at last, when the sun was sinking, the dogs were close upon the panting deer, and the prince believed he was about to secure his game, when the deer suddenly disappeared through the mouth of a cave which opened before him. The dogs followed at his heels, and the prince endeavoured to rein in his steed, but the impetuous animal bore him on, and soon was clattering over the stony floor of the cave in perfect darkness. Cuglas could hear ahead of him the cries of the hounds growing fainter and fainter, as they increased the distance between them and him. Then the cries ceased altogether, and the only sound the prince heard was the noise of his horse's hooves sounding in the hollow cave. Once more he endeavoured to check his career, but the reins broke in his hands, and in that instant the prince felt the horse had taken a plunge into a gulf, and was sinking down and down, as a stone cast from the summit of a cliff sinks down to the sea. At last the horse struck the ground again, and the prince was almost thrown out of his saddle, but he succeeded in regaining his seat. Then on through the darkness galloped the steed, and when he came into the light the prince's eyes were for some time unable to bear it. But when he got used to the brightness he saw he was galloping over a grassy plain, and in the distance he perceived the hounds rushing towards a wood faintly visible through a luminous summer haze. The prince galloped on, and as he approached the wood he saw coming towards him a comely champion, wearing a shining brown cloak, fastened by a bright bronze spear-like brooch, and bearing a white hazel wand in one hand, and a single-edged sword with a hilt made from the tooth of a sea-horse in the other;[8] and the prince knew by the dress of the champion and by his wand and sword, that he was a royal herald. As the herald came close to him the prince's steed stopped of his own accord.

'You are welcome, Cuglas,' said the herald, 'and I have been sent by the Princess Crede to greet you and to lead you to her court, where you have been so long expected.'

'I know not how this may be,' said Cuglas.

'How it has come about I shall tell you as we go along,' said the herald. 'The Princess Crede is the Queen of the Floating Island. And it chanced, once upon a day, when she was visiting her fairy kinsmen, who dwell in one of the pleasant hills that lie near Tara, she saw you with the high king and princes and nobles of Erin following the chase. And seeing you her heart went out to you, and wishing to bring you to her court, she sent one of her nymphs, in the form of a deer, to lure you on through the cave, which is the entrance to this land.'

'I am deeply honoured by the preference shown me by the princess,' said Cuglas, 'but I may not tarry in her court; for above in Erin there is the Lady Ailinn, the loveliest of all the ladies who grace the royal palace, and before the princes and chiefs of Erin she has promised to be my bride.'

'Of that I know not,' said the herald; 'but a true champion, like you, cannot, I know, refuse to come with me to the court of the Princess Crede.'

As the herald had said these words the prince

and he were on the verge of the wood, and they entered upon a mossy pathway that broadened out as they advanced until it was as wide as one of the great roads of Erin. Before they had gone very far the prince heard the tinkling of silver bells in the distance, and almost as soon as he heard them he saw coming up towards him a troop of warriors on coal black steeds. All the warriors wore helmets of shining silver, and cloaks of blue silk. And on the horses' breasts were crescents of silver, on which were hung tiny silver bells, shaking out music with the motion of the horses. As the prince approached the champions they lowered their spears, and dividing in two lines the prince and the herald passed between the ranks, and the champions, forming again, followed on behind the prince.

At last they passed through the wood, and they found themselves on a green plain, speckled with flowers, and they had not gone far when the prince saw coming towards him a hundred champions on snow-white steeds, and around the breasts of the steeds were crescents of gold, from which were hanging little golden bells.[9] The warriors all wore golden helmets, and the shafts of their shining spears were of gold, and golden sandals on their feet, and yellow silken mantles fell down over their shoulders. And when the prince came near them they lowered their lances, and then they turned their horses' heads around and marched before him. And it was not long until above the pleasant jingle of the bells the prince heard the measured strains of music, and he saw coming towards him a band of harpers, dressed in green and gold, and when the harpers had saluted the prince they marched in front of the cavalcade, playing all the time, and it was not long until they came to a stream that ran like a blue riband around the foot of a green hill, on the top of which was a sparkling palace; the stream was crossed by a golden bridge, so narrow that the horsemen had to go two-by-two. The herald asked the prince to halt and to allow all the champions to go before him; and the cavalcade ascended the hill, the sunlight brightly glancing on helmet and on lance, and when it reached the palace the horsemen filed around the walls.

When at length the prince and herald crossed the bridge and began to climb the hill, the prince thought he felt the ground moving under them, and on looking back he could see no sign of the golden bridge, and the blue stream had already become as wide as a great river, and was becoming wider every second.

'You are on the floating island now,' said the herald, 'and before you is the palace of the Princess Crede.'

At that moment the queen came out through the palace door, and the prince was so dazzled by her beauty, that only for the golden bracelet he wore upon his right arm, under the sleeve of his silken tunic, he might almost have forgotten the Princess Ailinn. This bracelet was made by the dwarfs who dwell in the heart of the Scandinavian Mountains, and was sent with other costly presents by the King of Scandinavia to the King of Erin, and he gave it to the princess, and it was the virtue of this bracelet, that whoever was wearing it could not forget the person who gave it to him, and it could never be loosened from the arm by any art or magic spell, but if the wearer, even for a single moment, liked anyone better than the person who gave it to him, that very moment the bracelet fell off from the arm and could never again be fastened on. And when the princess promised her hand in marriage to the Prince Cuglas, she closed the bracelet on his arm.

The fairy queen knew nothing about the bracelet, and she hoped that before the prince was long in the floating island he would forget all about the princess.

'You are welcome, Cuglas,' said the queen, as she held out her hand, and Cuglas, having thanked her for her welcome, they entered the palace together.

'You must be weary after your long journey,' said the queen. 'My page will lead you to your apartments, where a bath of the cool blue waters of the lake has been made ready for you, and when you have taken your bath the pages will lead you to the banquet-hall, where the feast is spread.'

At the feast the prince was seated beside the queen, and she talked to him of all the pleasures that were in store for him in fairyland, where pain, and sickness, and sorrow, and old age, are unknown, and where every rosy hour that flies is brighter than the one that has fled before it. And when the feast was ended the queen opened the dance with the prince, and it was not until the moon was high above the floating island that the prince retired to rest.

He was so tired after his journey and the dancing that he fell into a sound sleep. When he awoke the next morning the sun was shining brightly, and he heard outside the palace the jingle of bells and the music of baying hounds, and his heart was stirred by memories of the many pleasant days on which he had led the chase over the plains and through the green woods of Tara.

He looked out through the window, and he saw all the fairy champions mounted on their steeds ready for the chase, and at their head the fairy queen. And at that moment the pages came to say the queen wished to know if he would join them, and the prince went out and found his steed ready saddled and bridled, and they spent the day hunting in the forest that stretched away for miles behind the palace, and the night in feasting and dancing.

When the prince awoke the following morning he was summoned by the pages to the presence of the queen. The prince found the queen on the lawn outside the palace surrounded by her court.

'We shall go on the lake today, Cuglas,' said the queen, and taking his arm she led him along the water's edge, all the courtiers following.

When she was close to the water she waved her wand, and in a second a thousand boats, shining like glass, shot up from the beneath the lake and set their bows against the bank. The queen and Cuglas stepped into one, and when they were seated two fairy harpers took their places in the prow. All the other boats were soon thronged by fairies, and then the queen waved her wand again, and an awning of purple silk rose over the boat, and silken awning of various colours over the others, and the royal boat moved off from the bank followed by all the rest, and in every boat sat a harper with a golden harp, and when the queen waved her wand for the third time, the harpers struck the trembling chords, and to the sound of the delightful music the boats glided over the sunlit lake. And on they went until they approached the mouth of a gentle river sliding down between banks clad with trees. Up the river, close to the bank and under the drooping trees, they sailed, and when they came to a bend in the river, from which the lake could be no longer seen, they pushed their prows in against the bank, and the queen and Cuglas, and all the party, left the boats and went on under the trees until they came to a mossy glade.

Then the queen waved her wand, and silken couches were spread under the trees, and she and Cuglas sat on one apart from the others, and the courtiers took their places in proper order.

And the queen waved her wand again, and wind shook the trees above them, and the most luscious fruit that was ever tasted fell down into their hands; and when the feast was over there was dancing in the glades to the music of the harps, and when they were tired dancing they set out for the boats, and the moon was rising above the trees as they sailed away over the lake, and it was not long until they reached the bank below the fairy palace.

Well, between hunting in the forest, and sailing over the lake, and dancing in the greenwood glade and in the banquet-hall, the days passed, but all the time the prince was thinking of the Princess Ailinn, and one moonlit night, when he was lying awake on his couch thinking of her, a shadow was suddenly cast on the floor.

The prince looked towards the window, and what should he see sitting on the sill outside but a little woman tapping the pane with a golden bodkin.

The prince jumped from his couch and opened the window, and the little woman floated on the moonbeams into the room and sat down on the floor.

'You are thinking of the Princess Ailinn,' said the little woman.

'I never think of anyone else,' said the prince.

'I know that,' said the little woman, 'and it's because of your love for each other, and because her mother was a friend to me in the days gone by, that I have come here to try and help you; but there is not much time for talking, the night advances. At the bank below a boat awaits you. Step into it and it will lead you to the mainland, and when you reach it you will find before you a path that will take you to the green fields of Erin and the plains of Tara. I know you will have to face danger. I know not what kind of danger; but whatever it may be do not draw your sword before you tread on the mainland, for if you do you shall never reach it, and the boat will come back again to the floating island; and now go and may luck go with you;' and saying this the little woman climbed up the moonbeams and disappeared.

The prince left the palace and descended to the lake, and there before him he saw a glistening boat; he stepped into it, and the boat went on and on beneath the moon, and at last he saw the mainland, and he could trace a winding pathway going away from the shore. The sight filled his heart with joy, but suddenly the milk-white moonshine died away, and looking up to the sky he saw the moon turning fiery red, and the waters of the lake, shining like silver a moment before, took a blood-red hue, and a wind arose that stirred the waters, and they leaped up against the little boat, tossing it from side to side. While Cuglas was wondering at the change, he heard a strange, unearthly noise ahead of him, and a bristling monster, lifting its claws above the water, in a moment was beside the boat and stuck one of his claws in the left arm of the prince, and pierced the flesh to the bone. Maddened by the pain the prince drew his sword and chopped off the monster's claw. The monster disappeared beneath the lake, and, as it did so, the colour of the water changed, and the silver moonlight shone down from the sky again, but the boat no longer went on towards the mainland, but sped back towards the floating island, while forth from the island came a fleet of fairy boats to meet it, led by the shallop of the fairy queen. The queen greeted the prince as if she knew not of his attempted flight, and to the music of the harps the fleet returned to the palace.

The next day passed and the night came, and again the prince was lying on the couch, thinking of the Princess Ailinn, and again he saw the shadow on the floor and heard the tapping against the window.

And when he opened it the little woman slid into the room.

'You failed last night,' said she. 'but I come to give you another chance. Tomorrow the queen must set out on a visit to her fairy kinsmen, who dwell in the green hill near the plain of Tara; she cannot take you with her, for if your feet once touched the green grass that grows in the fruitful fields of Erin, she could never bring you back again. And so, when you find she has left the palace, go at once into the banquet-hall and look behind the throne, and you will see a small door let down into the ground. Pull this up and descend the steps

94

which you will see. Where they lead to I cannot tell. What dangers may be before you I do not know; but this I know, if you accept anything, no matter what it is, from anyone you may meet on your way, you shall not set foot on the soil of Erin.'

And having said this the little woman, rising from the floor, floated out through the window.

The prince returned to his couch, and the next morning, as soon as he heard the queen had left the palace, he hastened to the banquet-hall. He discovered the door and descended the steps, and he found himself in a gloomy and lonesome valley. Jagged mountains, black as night, rose on either side, and huge rocks seemed ready to topple down upon him at every step. Through broken clouds a watery moon shed a faint, fitful light, that came and went as the clouds, driven by a moaning wind, passed over the valley.

Cuglas, nothing daunted, pushed on boldly until a bank of cloud shut out completely the struggling moon, and closing over the valley covered it like a pall, leaving him in perfect darkness. At the same moment the moaning wind died away, and with it died away all sound. The darkness and the death-like silence sent an icy chill to the heart of Cuglas. He held his hand close to his eyes, but he saw it not. He shouted that he might hear the sound of his own voice, but he heard it not. He stamped his foot on the rocky ground, but no sound was returned to him. He rattled his sword in its brazen scabbard, but it gave no answer back to him. His heart grew colder and colder, when suddenly the cloud above him was rent in a dozen places, and lightning flashed through the valley, and the thunder rolled over the echoing mountains. In the lurid glare of the lightning Cuglas saw a hundred ghostly forms sweeping towards him, uttering as they came nearer and nearer shrieks so terrible that the silence of death could more easily be borne. Cuglas turned to escape, but they hemmed him round, and pressed their clammy hands upon his face.

With a yell of horror he drew his sword and slashed about him, and that very moment the forms vanished, the thunder ceased, the dark cloud passed, and the sun shone out as bright as on a summer day, and then Cuglas knew the forms he had seen were those of the wild people of the glen.[10]

With renewed courage he pursued his way through the valley, and after three or four windings it took him out upon a sandy desert. He had no sooner set foot upon the desert than he heard behind him a crashing sound louder than thunder. He looked around, and he saw that the walls of mountain through which he had just passed had fallen into the valley, and filled it up so that he could no longer tell where it had been.

The sun was beating fiercely on the desert, and the sands were almost as hot as burning cinders; and as Cuglas advanced over them his body became dried up, and his tongue clove to the roof of his mouth, and when his thirst was at its height a fountain of sparkling water sprang up in the burning plain a few paces in front of him; but when he came up quite close to it and stretched out his parched hands to cool them in the limped waters, the fountain vanished as suddenly as it appeared. With great pain, and almost choking with heat and thirst, he struggled on, and again the fountain sprang up in front of him and moved before him, almost within his reach. At last he came to the end of the desert, and he saw a green hill up which a pathway climbed; but as he came to the foot of the hill, there, sitting right in his way, was a beautiful fairy holding out towards him a crystal cup, over the rim of which flowed water as clear as crystal. Unable to resist the temptation, the prince seized the cold, bright goblet, and drank the water. When he did so his thirst vanished, but the fairy, and the green hill, and the burning desert disappeared, and he was standing in the forest behind the palace of the fairy queen.

That evening the queen returned, and at the feast she talked as gaily to the prince as if she knew not of his attempt to leave the Floating Island, and the prince spoke as gaily as he could to her, although in his heart there was sadness when he remembered that if he had only dashed away the crystal cup, he would be at that moment in the royal banquet-hall of Tara, sitting beside the Princess Ailinn.

And he thought the feast would never end; but it was over at last, and the prince returned to his apartments. And that night, as he lay on his couch, he kept his eyes fixed upon the window; but hours passed, and there was no sign of anyone. At long last, and when he had given up all hope of seeing her, he heard a tapping at the window, and he got up and opened it, and the little woman came in.

'You failed again today,' said she — 'failed just at the very moment when you were about to step on the green hills of Erin. I can give you only one chance more. It will be your last. The queen will go hunting in the morning. Join the hunt, and when you are separated from the rest of the party in the wood throw your reins upon your horse's neck and he will lead you to the edge of the lake. Then cast this golden bodkin into the lake in the direction of the mainland, and a golden bridge will be thrown across, over which you can pass safely to the fields of Erin; but take care and do not draw your sword, for if you do your steed will bear you back again to the Floating Island, and here you must remain for ever.' Then handing the bodkin to the prince, and saying goodbye, the little woman disappeared.

The next morning the queen and the prince and all the court went out to hunt, and a fleet white deer started out before them, and the royal party pressed after him in pursuit. The prince's steed outstripped the others, and when he was alone the prince flung the reins upon his horse's neck, and before long he came to the edge of the lake.

Then the prince cast the bodkin onto the water, and a golden bridge was thrown across to the mainland, and the horse galloped onto it, and when the prince was more than half-way he saw riding towards him a champion wearing a silver helmet, and carrying on his left arm a silver shield, and holding in his right hand a gleaming sword. As he came nearer he struck his shield with his sword and challenged the prince to battle. The prince's sword almost leaped out of its scabbard at the martial sound, and, like a true knight of Tara, he dashed against his foe, and swinging his sword above his head, with one blow he clove the silver helmet, and the strange warrior reeled from his horse and fell upon the golden bridge. The prince content with this achievement, spurred his horse to pass the fallen champion, but the horse refused to stir, and the bridge broke in two almost at his feet, and the part of it between him and the mainland disappeared beneath the lake, carrying with it the horse and the body of the champion, and before the prince could recover from his surprise, his steed wheeled round and was galloping back, and when he reached the land he rushed through the forest, and the prince was not able to pull him up until he came to the palace door.

All that night the prince lay awake on his couch with his eyes fixed upon the window, but no shadow fell upon the floor, and there was no tapping at the pane, and with a heavy heart he joined the hunting party in the morning. And day followed day, and his heart was sadder and sadder, and found no pleasure in the joys and delights of fairyland. And when all in the palace were at rest he used to roam through the forest, always thinking of the Princess Ailinn, and hoping against hope that the little woman would come again to him, but at last he began to despair of ever seeing her. It chanced one night he rambled so far that he found himself on the verge of the lake, at the very spot from which the golden bridge had been thrown across the waters, and as he gazed wistfully upon them a boat shot up and came swiftly to the bank, and who should he see sitting in the stern but the little woman.

'Ah Cuglas, Cuglas,' she said, 'I gave you three chances, and you failed in all of them.'

'I should have borne the pain inflicted by the monster's claw,' said Cuglas. 'I should have borne the thirst of the sandy desert, and dashed the crystal cup untasted from the fairy's hand; but I could never have faced the nobles and chiefs of

Erin if I had refused to meet the challenge of the battle champion on the golden bridge.'

'And you would have been no true knight of Erin, and you would not have been worthy of the wee girl who loves you, the bonny Princess Ailinn, if you had refused to meet it,' said the little woman; 'but for all that you can never return to the fair hills of Erin. But cheer up, Cuglas, there are mossy ways and forest paths and nestling bowers in fairyland. Lonely they are, I know, in your eyes now,' said the little woman; 'but maybe,' she added, with a laugh as musical as the ripple on a streamlet when summer is in the air, 'maybe you won't always think them so lonely.'

'You think I'll forget Ailinn for the fairy queen,' said Cuglas, with a sigh.

'I don't think anything of the kind,' said she.

'Then what do you mean?' said the prince.

'Oh, I mean what I mean,' said the little woman. 'But I can't stop here all night talking to you; and, indeed, it is in your bed you ought to be yourself. So now good night; and I have no more to say, except that perhaps, if you happen to be here this night week at this very hour, when the moon will be on the waters, you will see —. But no matter what you will see,' said she; 'I must be off.'

And before the prince could say another word the boat sped away from the bank, and he was alone. He went back to the palace, and he fell asleep that night only to dream of the Princess Ailinn.

As for the princess, she was pining away in the palace of Tara, the colour had fled from her cheeks, and her eyes, which had been once so bright they would have lighted darkness like a star, lost nearly all their lustre, and the king's leeches could do nothing for her, and at last they gave up all hope, and the king and queen of Erin and the ladies of the court watched her couch by night and by day sadly waiting for her last hour.

At length one day, when the sun was shining brightly over Tara's plain, and its light, softened by the intervening curtains, was falling in the sick chamber, the royal watchers noticed a sweet change coming over the face of the princess; the bloom of love and youth were flushing on her cheeks, and from her eyes shone out the old, soft, tender light, and they began to hope she was about to be restored to them, when suddenly the room was in darkness as if the night had swept across the sky, and blotted out the sun. Then they heard the sound of fairy music, and over the couch where the princess lay they beheld a gleam of golden light, but only for a moment; and again there was perfect darkness, and the fairy music ceased. Then, as suddenly as it came the darkness vanished, the softened sunlight once more filled the chamber, and rested upon the couch; but the couch was empty, and the royal watchers, looking at each other, said in whispers; 'The fairies have carried away the Princess Ailinn to fairyland.'

Well, that very day the prince roamed by himself through the forest, counting the hours until the day would fade in the sky and the moon come climbing up, and at last, when it was shining full above the waters, he went down to the verge of the lake, and he looked out over the gleaming surface watching for the vision promised by the little woman. But he could see nothing, and was about to turn away when he heard the faint sound of fairy music. He listened and listened, and the sound came nearer and clearer, and away in the distance, like drops of glistening water breaking the level of the lake, he saw a fleet of fairy boats, and he thought it was the fairy queen sailing in the moonlight. And it was the fairy queen, and soon he was able to recognise the royal shallop leading the others, and as it came close to the bank he saw the little woman sitting in the prow between the little harpers, and at the stern was the fairy queen, and by her side the lady of his heart, the Princess Ailinn. In a second the boat was against the bank, and the princess in his arms. And he kissed her again and again.

'And have you never a kiss for me,' said the little woman, tapping his hand with the little gold bodlkin.

'A kiss and a dozen,' said Cuglas, as he caught the little fairy up in his arms.

'Oh, fie, Cuglas,' said the queen.

'Oh, the princess isn't one bit jealous,' said the little woman. 'Are you, Ailinn?'

'Indeed I am not,' said Ailinn.

'And you should not be,' said the fairy queen, 'for never lady yet had truer knight than Cuglas. I loved him, and I love him dearly. I lured him here hoping that in the delights of fairyland he might forget you. It was all in vain. I know now that there is one thing no fairy power above or below the stars, or beneath the waters, can ever subdue, and that is love. And here together forever shall you and Cuglas dwell, where old age shall never come upon you, and where pain or sorrow or sickness are unknown.'

And Cuglas never returned to the fair hills of

Erin, and ages passed away since the morning he followed the hounds into the fatal cave, but his story was remembered by the firesides, and sometimes, even yet, the herdboy watching his cattle in the fields hears the tuneful cry of hounds, and follows it till it leads him to a darksome cave, and as fearfully he listens to the sound becoming fainter and fainter he hears the clatter of hoofs over the stony floor, and to this day the cave bears the name of the prince who entered it never to return.*

* *Uaimh Belaigh Conglais*, the cave of the road of Cuglas — now Baltinglass — in the county Wicklow.

THE HUNTSMAN'S SON

A long, long time ago there lived in a little hut on the borders of a great forest a huntsman and his wife and son. From his earliest years the boy, whose name was Fergus, used to hunt with his father in the forest, and he grew up strong and active, sure and swift-footed as a deer, and as free and fearless as the wind. He was tall and handsome; as supple as a mountain ash, his lips were as red as its berries; his eyes were as blue as the skies in spring; and his hair fell down over his shoulders like a shower of gold. His heart was as light as a bird's, and no bird was fonder of green woods and waving branches. He had lived since his birth in the hut in the forest, and had never wished to leave it, until one winter night a wandering minstrel sought shelter there, and paid for his night's lodging with songs of love and battle. Ever since that night Fergus pined for another life. He no longer found joy in the music of the hounds or in the cries of the huntsmen in forest glades. He yearned for the chance of battle, and the clang of shields, and the fierce shouts of fighting warriors, and he spent all his spare hours practising on the harp and learning the use of arms, for in those days the bravest warriors were also bards. In this way the spring and summer and autumn passed; and when the winter came again it chanced that on a stormy night, when the thunder was rattling through the forest, smiting the huge oaks and hurling them crashing to the earth, Fergus lay awake thinking of his present lot, and wondering what the future might have in store for him. The lightning was playing around the hut, and every now and then a flash brightened up the interior.

After a peal, louder than any which had preceded it, Fergus heard three loud knocks at the door. He called out to his parents that someone was knocking.

'If that is so,' said his father, 'open at once; this is no night to keep a poor wanderer outside our door.'

Fergus did as he was bidden, and as he opened the door as flash of lightning showed him, standing at the threshold, a little wizened old man with a small harp under his arm.

'Come in, and welcome,' said Fergus, and the little man stepped into the room.

'It is a wild night, neighbours,' said he.

'It is, indeed, a wild night,' said the huntsman and his wife, who had got up and dressed themselves; 'and sorry we are we have no better shelter or better fare to offer you, but we give you the best we have.'

'A king cannot do more than his best,' said the little man.

The huntsman's wife lit the fire, and soon the pine logs flashed up into a blaze, and made the hut bright and warm. She then brought forth a peggin of milk and a cake of barley-bread.

'You must be hungry, sir,' she said.

'Hungry I am,' said he; 'but I wouldn't ask for better fare than this if I were in the king's palace.'

'Thank you kindly, sir,' said she, 'and I hope you will eat enough, and that it will do you good.'

'And while you are eating your supper,' said the huntsman, 'I'll make you a bed of fresh rushes.'

'Don't put yourself to that trouble,' said the little man. 'When I have done my supper I'll lie down here by the fire, if it is pleasing to you, and I'll sleep like a top until morning. And now go back to your beds and leave me to myself, and maybe some time when you won't be expecting it I'll do a good turn for your kindness to the poor wayfarer.'

'Oh, it's no kindness at all,' said the huntsman's wife. 'It would be a queer thing if an Irish cabin would not give shelter and welcome in a wild night like this. So good night, now, and we hope you will sleep well.'

'Good night,' said the little man, 'and may you and yours never sup sorrow until your dying day.'

The huntsman and his wife and Fergus then went back to their beds, and the little man, having finished his supper, curled himself up by the fire, and was soon fast asleep.

About an hour after a loud clap of thunder awakened Fergus, and before it had died away he heard three knocks at the door. He aroused his parents and told them.

'Get up at once,' said his mother, 'this is no night to keep a stranger outside our door.'

Fergus rose and opened the door, and a flash of lightning showed him a little old woman, with a shuttle in her hand, standing outside.

'Come in, and welcome,' said he, and the little old woman stepped into the room.

'Blessings be on them who give welcome to a wanderer on a wild night like this,' said the old woman.

'And who wouldn't give welcome on a night like this?' said the huntsman's wife, coming forward with a peggin of milk and a barley cake in her hand, 'and sorry we are we have not better fare to offer you.'

'Enough is as good as a feast,' said the little woman, 'and now go back to your beds and leave me to myself.'

'Not till I shake down a bed of rushes for you,' said the huntsman's wife.

'Don't mind the rushes,' said the little woman; 'go back to your beds. I'll sleep here by the fire.'

The huntsman's wife went to bed, and the little old woman, having eaten her supper, lay down by the fire, and was soon fast asleep.

About an hour later another clap of thunder startled Fergus. Again he heard three knocks at the door. He roused his parents, but he did not wait for orders from them. He opened the door, and a flash of lightning showed him outside the threshold a low-sized, shaggy, wild-looking horse. And Fergus knew it was the Pooka, the wild horse of the mountains. Bold as Fergus was, his heart beat quickly as he saw fire issuing from the Pooka's nostrils. But, banishing fear, he cried out:

'Come in, and welcome.'

'Welcome you are,' said the huntsman, 'and sorry we are that we have not better shelter or fare to offer you.'

'I couldn't wish a better welcome,' said the Pooka, as he came over near the fire and sat down on his haunches.

'Maybe you would like a bit of this, Master Pooka,' said the huntsman's wife, as she offered him a barley cake.

'I never tasted anything sweeter in my life,' said the Pooka, crunching it between his teeth, 'and now if you can give me a sup of milk, I'll want for nothing.'

The huntsman's wife brought him a peggin of milk. When he had drunk it, 'Now,' says the Pooka, 'go back to your beds, and I'll curl myself up by the fire and sleep like a top till morning.'

And soon everybody in the hut was fast asleep.

When the morning came the storm had gone, and the sun was shining through the windows of the hut. At the song of the lark Fergus got up, and no one in the world was ever more surprised than he when he saw no sign of the little old man, or the little old woman, or the wild horse of the mountains. His parents were also surprised, and they all thought that they must have been dreaming until they saw the empty peggins around the fire and some pieces of broken bread; and they did not know what to think of it all.

From that day forward the desire grew stronger in the heart of Fergus for a change of life; and one day he told his parents that he was resolved to seek his fortune. He said he wished to be a soldier, and that he would set out for the king's palace, and try to join the ranks of the Feni.

About a week afterwards he took leave of his parents, and having received their blessing he struck out for the road that led to the palace of the High King of Erin. He arrived there just at the time when the great captain of the Fenian host was recruiting his battalions, which had been thinned in recent battle.

The manly figure of Fergus, his gallant bearing, and handsome face, all told in his favour. But before he could be received into the Fenian ranks he had to prove that he could play the harp like a bard, that he could contend with staff and shield against nine Fenian warriors, that he could run with plaited hair through the tangled forest without loosening a single hair, and that in his course he could jump over trees as high as his head, and stoop under trees as low as his knee, and that he could run so lightly that the rotten twig should not break under his feet. Fergus proved equal to all the tests, thanks to the wandering minstrel who taught him the use of the harp, to his own brave heart, and to his forest training. He was enrolled in the second battalion of the Feni, and before long he was its bravest and ablest champion.

At that very time it happened that the niece of the High King of Erin was staying with the king and queen in their palace at Tara. The princess was the loveliest lady in all the land. She was as proud as she was beautiful. The princes and chieftains of Erin in vain sought her hand in marriage. From Alba and Spain, and the far-off isles of Greece, kings came to woo her. From the northern lands came vikings in stately galleys with brazen prows, whose oarsmen tore the white foam from the emerald seas as they swept towards the Irish coasts. But the lady had vowed she would wed with no one except a battle champion who could excel in music the chief bard of the High King of Erin; who could outstrip on his steed in the great race of Tara the white steed of the plains; and who could give her as a wedding robe a garment of all the colours of the rainbow, so finely spun that when folded up it would fit in the palm of her small white hand. To fulfil these three conditions was impossible for all her suitors, and it seemed as if the loveliest lady of the land should go unmarried to her grave.

It chanced that once, on a day when the Fenian battalions were engaged in a hurling-match, Fergus beheld the lady watching the match from her sunny bower. He no sooner saw her than he fell over head and ears in love with her, and he thought of her by night, and he thought of her by day, and believing that his love was hopeless, he often wished he had never left his forest-home.

The great fair of Tara[11] was coming on, and all the Feni were busy from morning till night practising feats of arms and games, in order to take part in the contests to be held during the fair. And Fergus, knowing that the princess would be present, determined to do his best to win the prizes which were to be contended for before the ladies' eyes.

The fair began on the 1st August, but for a whole week before the five great roads of Erin were thronged with people of all sorts. Princes and warriors on their steeds, battle champions in their chariots, harpers in hundreds, smiths with gleaming spears and shields and harness for battle steeds and chariots; troops of men and boys leading race-horses; jewellers with gold drinking-horns, and brooches, and pins, and ear-rings, and costly gems of all kinds, and chess-boards of silver and gold, and golden and silver chessmen in bags of woven brass; dyers with their many-coloured fabrics; bands of jugglers; drovers goading on herds of cattle; shepherds driving their sheep; huntsmen with spoils of the chase; dwellers in the lakes or by the fish-abounding rivers with salmon and speckled trout; and countless numbers of peasants on horseback and on foot, all wending their way to the great meeting-place by the mound, which a thousand years before had been raised over the grave of the great queen. For there the fair was to be held.

On the opening day the High King, attended by the four kings of Erin, set out from the palace, and with them went the queen and ladies of the court in sparkling chariots. The princess rode in the chariot with the high queen, under an awning made of the wings of birds, to protect them from the rays of the sun. Following the queen were the court ladies in other chariots, under awnings of purple or of yellow silk. Then came the brehons, the great judges of the land, and the chief bards of the high court of Tara, and the Druids, crowned with oak leaves, and carrying wands of divination in their hands.

When the royal party reached the ground it took its place in enclosures right up against the monumental mound. The High King sat with the four kings of Erin, all wearing their golden helmets, for they wore their diadems in battle only. In an enclosure next the king's sat the queen and the princess and all the ladies of the court. At either side of the royal pavilions were others for the dames and ladies and nobles and chiefs of different degrees, forming part of a circle on the plain, and the stands and benches for the people were so arranged as to complete the circle, and in the round green space within it, so that all might hear and see, the contests were to take place.

At a signal from the king, who was greeted with a thunderous cheer, the heralds rode round the circle, and having struck their sounding shields three times with their swords, they made a solemn proclamation of peace. Then was sung by all the assembled bards, to the accompaniment of their harps, the chant in honour of the mighty dead. When this was ended, again the heralds struck their shields, and the contests began. The first contest was the contest of spear-throwing between the champions of the seven battalions of the Feni. When the seven champions took their places in front of the royal enclosure, everyone, even the proud princess, was struck by the manly beauty and noble bearing of Fergus.

The champions poised their spears, and at a stroke from the heralds upon their shields the seven spears sped flashing through the air. They all struck the ground, shafts up, and it was seen that two were standing side by side in advance of the rest, one belonged to Fergus, the other to the great chief, Oscar. The contest for the prize then lay between Oscar and Fergus, and when they stood in front of the king, holding their spears aloft, every heart was throbbing with excitement. Once more the heralds struck their shields, and, swifter than the lightning's flash, forth went the spears, and when Fergus's spear was seen shivering in the ground a full length ahead of the great chief Oscar's, the air was shaken by a wild cheer that was heard far beyond the plains of Tara. And as Fergus approached the high king to receive the prize the cheers were renewed. But Fergus thought more of the winsome glance of the princess than he did of the prize or the sounding cheers. And Princess Maureen was almost sorry for her vow, for her heart was touched by the beauty of the Fenian champion.

Other contests followed, and the day passed, and the night fell, and while the Fenian warriors were revelling in their camps, the heart of Fergus, victor as he was, was sad and low. He escaped from his companions, and stole away to his native forest, for —

When the heart is sick and sorest,
There is balsam in the forest —
There is balsam in the forest
For its pain.

And as he lay under the spreading branches, watching the stars glancing through the leaves, and listening to the slumb'rous murmur of the waters, a strange peace came over him.

But in the camp which he had left, and in the vast multitude on the plains of Tara, there was stir and revelry, and babbling speculation as to the contest of tomorrow — the contest which was to decide whether the chief bard of Erin was to hold his own against all comers, or yield the palm. For rumour said that a great Skald had come from the northern lands to compete with the Irish bard.

At last, over the Fenian camp, and over the great plain and the multitude that thronged it, sleep fell, clothing them with a silence as deep as that which dwelt in the forest, where, dreaming of the princess, Fergus lay. He awoke at the first notes of the birds, but though he felt he ought to go back to his companions and be witness of the contest which might determine whether the princess was to be another's bride, his great love and his utter despair of winning her so oppressed him that he lay as motionless as a broken reed. He scarcely heard the music of the birds, and paid no heed to the murmur of the brook rushing by his feet. The crackling of branches near him barely disturbed him, but when a shadow fell across his eyes he looked up gloomily, and saw, or thought he saw, someone standing before him. He started up, and who should he see but the little wizened old man who found shelter in his father's hut on the stormy night.

'This is a nice place for a battle champion to be. This is a nice place for *you* to be on the day which is to decide who will be the successful suitor of the princess.'

'What is it to me,' said Fergus, 'who is to win her since I cannot.'

'I told you,' said the little man, 'the night you opened the door for me, that the time might come when I might be able to do a good turn for you and yours. The time has come. Take this harp, and my luck go with you, and in the contest of the bards today you'll reap the reward of the kindness you did when you opened your door to the poor old wayfarer in the midnight storm.'

The little man handed his harp to Fergus and disappeared as swiftly as the wind that passes through the leaves.

Fergus, concealing the harp under his silken cloak, reached the camp before his comrades had aroused themselves from sleep.

At length the hour arrived when the great contest was to take place.

The king gave the signal, and as the chief bard of Erin was seen ascending the mound in front of the royal enclosures he was greeted with a roar of cheers, but at the first note of his harp silence like that of night fell on the mighty gathering.

As he moved his fingers softly over the strings every heart was hushed, filled with a sense of balmy rest. The lark soaring and singing above his head paused mute and motionless in the still air, and no sound was heard over the spacious plain save the dreamy music. Then the bard struck another key, and a gentle sorrow possessed the hearts of his hearers, and unbidden tears gathered to their eyes. Then, with bolder hand, he swept his fingers across his lyre, and all hearts were moved to joy and pleasant laughter, and eyes that had been dimmed by tears sparkled as brightly as running waters dancing in the sun. When the last notes had died away a cheer arose, loud as the voice of the storm in the glen when the live thunder is revelling on the mountain tops. As soon as the bard had descended the mound the Skald from the northern lands took his place, greeted by cries of welcome from a hundred thousand throats. He touched his harp, and in the perfect silence was heard the strains of the mermaid's song, and through it the pleasant ripple of summer waters on the pebbly beach. Then the theme was changed, and on the air was borne the measured sweep of countless oars and the swish of waters around the prows of contending galleys, and the breezy voices of the sailors and the sea-bird's cry. Then his theme was changed to the mirth and laughter of the banquet-hall, the clang of meeting drinking-horns, and the songs of battle. When the last strain ended, from the mighty host a great shout went up, loud as the roar of winter billows breaking in the hollows of the shore; and men knew not whom to declare the victor, the chief bard of Erin or the Skald of the northern lands.

In the height of the debate the cry arose that another competitor had ascended the mound, and there standing in view of all was Fergus, the huntsman's son. All eyes were fastened upon him, but no one looked so eagerly as the princess.

115

He touched his harp with gentle fingers, and a sound low and soft as a faint summer breeze passing through forest trees stole out, and then was heard the rustle of birds through the branches, and the dreamy murmur of waters lost in deepest woods, and all the fairy echoes whispering when the leaves are motionless in the noonday heat; then followed notes cool and soft as the drip of summer showers on the parched grass, and then the song of the blackbird, sounding as clearly as it sounds in long silent spaces of the evening, and then in one sweet jocund burst the multitudinous voices that hail the breaking of the morn. And the lark, singing and soaring above the minstrel, sank mute and motionless upon his shoulder, and from all the leafy woods the birds came thronging out and formed a fluttering canopy above his head.

When the bard ceased playing no shout arose from the mighty multitude, for the strains of his harp, long after its chords were stilled, held their hearts spell-bound.

And when he had passed away from the mound of contest all knew there was no need to declare the victor.[12] And all were glad the comely Fenian champion had maintained the supremacy of the bards of Erin. But there was one heart sad, the heart of the princess; and now she wished more than ever that she had never made her hateful vow.

Other contests went on, but Fergus took no interest in them; and once more he stole away to the forest glade. His heart was sorrowful, for he thought of the great race of the morning, and he knew that he could not hope to compete with the rider of the white steed of the plains. And as he lay beneath the spreading branches during the whole

116

night long his thoughts were not of the victory he had won, but of the princess, who was as far away from him as ever. He passed the night without sleep, and when the morning came he rose and walked aimlessly through the woods.

A deer starting from a thicket reminded him of the happy days of his boyhood, and once more the wish came back to him that he had never left his forest home. As his eyes followed the deer wistfully, suddenly he started in amazement. The deer vanished from view, and in his stead was the wild horse of the mountains.

'I told you I'd do you a good turn,' said the Pooka, 'for the kindness you and yours did me on that wild winter's night. The day is passing. You have no time to lose. The white steed of the plains is coming to the starting-post. Jump on my back, and remember, "Faint heart never won fair lady".'

In half a second Fergus was bestride the Pooka, whose coat of shaggy hair became at once as glossy as silk, and just at the very moment when the king was about to declare there was no steed to compete with the white steed of the plains, the Pooka with Fergus upon his back, galloped up in front of the royal enclosure. When the people saw the champion a thunderous shout rose up that startled the birds in the skies, and sent them flying to the groves.

And in the ladies' enclosure was a rustle of many-coloured scarves waving in the air. At the striking of the shields the contending steeds rushed from the post with the swiftness of a swallow's flight. But before the white steed of the plains had gone half-way round, Fergus and the wild horse of the mountains had passed the winning post, greeted by

117

such cheers as had never before been heard on the plains of Tara.

Fergus heard the cheers, but scarcely heeded them, for his heart went out through his eyes that were fastened on the princess, and a wild hope stirred him that his glance was not ungrateful to the loveliest lady of the land.

And the princess was sad and sorry for her vow, for she believed that it was beyond the power of Fergus to bring her a robe of all the colours of the rainbow, so subtly woven as to fit in the palm of her soft, white hand.

That night also Fergus went to the forest, not too sad, because there was a vague hope in his heart that had never been there before. He lay down under the branches, with his feet towards the rustling waters, and the smiles of the princess gilded his slumbers, as the rays of the rising sun gild the glades of the forest; and when the morning came he was scarcely surprised when before him appeared the little old woman with the shuttle he had welcomed on the winter's night.

'You think you have won her already,' said the little woman. 'And so you have, too; her heart is all your own, and I'm half inclined to think that my trouble will be thrown away, for if you had never a wedding robe to give her, she'd rather have you this minute than all the kings of Erin, or than all the other princes and kings and chieftains in the whole world. But you and your father and mother were kind to me on a wild winter's night, and I'd never see your mother's son without a wedding robe fit for the greatest princess that ever set nations to battle for her beauty. So go and pluck me a handful of wild forest flowers, and I'll weave out of them a wedding robe with all the colours of the rainbow, and one that will be as sweet and as fragrant as the ripe, red lips of the princess herself.'

Fergus, with joyous heart, culled the flowers, and brought them to the little old woman.

In the twinkling of an eye she wove with her little shuttle a wedding robe, with the all the colours of the rainbow, as light as the fairy dew, as soft as the hand of the princess, as fragrant as her little red mouth, and so small that it would pass through the eye of a needle.

'Go now, Fergus,' said he, 'and may luck go with you; but, in the days of your greatness and of the glory which will come to you when you are wedded to the princess, be as kind, and have as open a heart and as open a door for the poor as you had when you were only a poor huntsman's son.'

Fergus took the robe and went towards Tara. It was the last day of the fair, and all the contests were over, and the bards were about to chant the farewell strains to the memory of the great queen. But before the chief bard could ascend the mound, Fergus, attended by a troop of Fenian warriors on their steeds, galloped into the enclosure, and rode up in front of the queen's pavilion. Holding up the glancing and many-coloured robe, he said:

'O Queen and King of Erin! I claim the princess for my bride. You, O king, have decided that I have won the prize in the contest of the bards; that I have won the prize in the race against the white steed of the plains; it is for the princess to say if the robe which I give her will fit in the hollow of her small white hand.'

'Yes,' said the king. 'You are victor in the contests; let the princess declare if you have fulfilled the last condition.'

The princess took the robe from Fergus, closed her fingers over it, so that no vestige of it was seen.

'Yes, O king!' said she, 'he has fulfilled the last condition; but before ever he had fulfilled a single one of them, my heart went out to the comely champion of the Feni. I was willing then, I am ready now, to become the bride of the huntsman's son.'

NOTES

1. *The Birds of the Mystic Lake.*

The incident of the birds coming to the mystic lake is taken from The Voyage of Maildun, a translation of which is given in Joyce's *Old Celtic Romances*. The operations of the birds were witnessed by Maildun and his companions, who, in the course of their wanderings, had arrived at the Isle of the Mystic Lake. One of Maildun's companions, Diuran, on seeing the wonder, said to the others: 'Let us bathe in the lake, and we shall obtain a renewal of our youth like the birds.'

But they said: 'No so, for the bird has left the poison of his old age and decay in the water.'

Diuran, however, plunged in, and swam about for some time; after which he took a little of the water and mixed it in his mouth, and in the end he swallowed a small quantity. He then came out perfectly sound and whole, and remained so ever after as long as he lived. But none of the others ventured in.

The return of the birds in the character of the cormorants of the western seas and guardians of the lake does not occur in the old tale. The oldest copy of the voyage is in *The Book of The Dun Cow* (about the year 1100). O'Curry says the voyage was undertaken about the year 700. It was made by Maildun in search of pirates who had slain his father. The story is full of fancy.

2. *The House in the Lake.*

In the Irish annals lake dwellings, which were formerly common in Ireland, are called *crannogs*, from crann, a tree, either because of the timber framework of which the island

121

was formed or of the wooden huts erected thereon.

Some *crannogs* appear to have been veritable islands, the only means of communication with the land being canoes. Remains of these have been frequently found near the dwelling, in some instances alongside the landing stage, as if sunk at their moorings.

'Favourite sites for *crannogs* were marshes, small loughs surrounded by woods and large sheets of water. As providing good fishing grounds the entrance to or exit of a stream from a lake was eagerly selected.' — *Lake Dwellings of Ireland*, Col. Wood Martin, M.R.I.A.

3. *Brian's Water-dress.*

Brian, Ur, and Urcar, the three sons of Turenn, were de Danaan chiefs. They slew Kian, the father of Luga of the Long Arms, who was grandson of Balor of the Evil Eye. Luga imposed an extraordinary *eric* fine on the sons of Turenn, part of which was 'the cooking-spit of the women of Fincara'. For a quarter of a year Brian and his brothers sailed hither and thither over the wide ocean, landing on many shores, seeking tidings of the Island of Fincara. At last they met a very old man, who told them that the island lay deep down in the waters, having been sunk beneath the waves by a spell in times long past.

Then Brian put on his water-dress, with his helmet of transparent crystal on his head, telling his brothers to wait his return. He leaped over the side of the ship, and sank at once out of sight. He walked about for a fortnight down in the green salt sea, seeking for the Island of Fincara, and at last he found it.

His brothers waited for him in the same spot the whole time, and when he came not they began to fear he would return no more. At last they were about to leave the place, when they saw the glitter of his crystal helmet deep down in the water, and immediately after he came to the surface with the cooking-spit in his hand. — *Old Celtic Romances* (Joyce), p. 87.

4. *The Palace of the Little Cat.*

The description of the rows of jewels ranged round the wall of the palace of the Little Cat is taken from *The Voyage of Maildun.* — See Note 1.

5. *Liban the Mermaid.*

Liban was the daughter of Ecca, son of Mario, King of Munster. Ecca, having conquered the lordship of the half of Ulster, settled down with his people in the plain of the Grey Copse, which is now covered by the waters of Lough Necca, now Lough Neagh. A magic well had sprung up in the plain, and not being properly looked after by the woman in charge of it, its waters burst forth over the plain, drowning Ecca and nearly all his family. Liban, although swept away like the others, was not drowned. She lived for a whole year, with her lap-dog, in a chamber beneath the lake, and God protected her from the water. At the end of that time she was weary, and when she saw the speckled salmon swimming and playing all round her, she prayed to be changed into a salmon that she might swim with the others through the green, salt sea. Her prayer was granted; she took the shape of a salmon, except her face and breast, which did not change. And her lap-dog was changed into an otter, and attended her afterwards whithersoever she went as long as she lived in the sea.

It is nearly eight hundred years ago since the story was transcribed from some old authority into the *Book of the Dun Cow*, the oldest manuscript of Gaelic literature we possess. — Joyce's *Old Celtic Romances*, p. 97.

6. *The Fairy Tree of Dooros.*

The forest of Dooros was in the district of Hy Fiera of the Moy (now the barony of Tireragh, in Sligo).

On a certain occasion the de Danaans, returning from a hurling match with the Feni, passed through the forest, carrying with them for food during the journey crimson nuts, and arbutus apples, and scarlet quicken-berries, which they had brought from the Land of Promise. One of the quicken-berries dropped on the earth, and the de Danaans passed on not heeding.

From this berry a great quicken-tree sprang up, which had the virtues of the quicken-trees that grow in fairyland. Its berries had the taste of honey, and those who ate of them felt a cheeful glow, as if they had drunk of wine or old mead, and if a man were even a hundred years old he returned to the age of thirty as soon as he had eaten three of them.

The de Danaans having heard of this tree, and not wishing that anyone should eat of the berries but themselves, sent a giant of their own people to guard it, namely, Sharvan the Surly, of Lochlann. — 'The Pursuit of Diarmuid and Grania', *Old Celtic Romances*, (Joyce), p. 313.

7. *Prince Cuglas.*

In the list of the historic tales mentioned in the *Book of Leinster*, and which is given in O'Curry's appendix to his *Lectures on the MSS. Materials of Ancient Irish History*, 'The Cave of the Road of Cuglas' finds place. O'Curry has the following note:

'Cuglas was the son of Donn Desa, King of Leinster, and master of the hounds to the monarch Conairé Mor. Having one day followed the chase from Tara to this road, the chase suddenly disappeared in a cave, into which he followed, and was *never seen after*. Hence the cave was called *Uaimh Bealach Conglais*, or the cave of the road of Cuglas (now Baltinglass, in the County of Wicklow). It is about this cave, nevertheless, that so many of our pretended Irish antiquarians have written so much nonsense in connection with some imaginary pagan worship to which they gravely assure the world, on entymological authority, the spot was devoted. The authority for the legend of Cuglas is the *Dinnoean Chus* on the place *Bealach Conglais (Book of Lecain)*. The full tale has not come down to us.'

8. *The Herald.*

'Here comes a single champion towards us, O *Cuchulain*,'

124

said *Laegh* (Cuchulain's charioteer). 'What sort of a champion is he?' said *Cuchulain.* 'A brown-haired, broad-faced, beautiful youth; a splendid brown cloak on him; a bright bronze spear-like brooch fastening his cloak. A full and well-fitting shirt to his skin. Two firm shoes between his two feet and the ground. A hand-staff of white hazel in one hand of his; a single-edged sword with a sea-horse hilt in his other hand.' 'Good, my lad,' said *Cuchulain;* 'these are the tokens of a herald,' — Description of the herald *MacRoath* in the story of the *Tain bo Chuaillgné.* — O'Curry's *Manners and Customs of the Ancient Irish*, Vol. II, p. 301.

9. *Golden Bells.*

In O'Curry's *Lectures on the Manners of Customs of the Ancient Irish* are several dazzling descriptions of calvacades taken from the old tales. Silver and golden bells are frequently mentioned as part of the horse furniture.

10. *The Wild People of the Glen.*

'And then he put on his helmet of battle and of combat and of fighting, from every recess and from every angle of which issued the shout as it were of a hundred warriors; because it was alike that woman of the valley (*de benanaig*), and hobgoblins (*becanaig*), and wild people of the glen (*geinti glindi*), and demons of the air (*demna acoir*), shouted in front of it, and in rear of it, and over it, and around it, wherever he went, at the spurting of blood, and of heroes upon it.'

Description of Cuchulain's helmet in the story of the *Tain bo Chuailgné.* — O'Curry's *Manners and Customs of the Ancient Irish*, Vol. II, p. 301.

11. *The Fair of Tara.*

'The great fairs anciently held in Ireland were not like their modern representatives, mere markets, but were assemblies of the people to celebrate funeral games, and other religious rites; during pagan times to hold parliaments, promulgate laws, listen to the recitation of tales and poems, engage in or witness contests in feats of arms, horse-racing, and other popular games. They were analogous in many ways to the Olympian and other celebrated games of ancient Greece.

These assemblies were regulated by a strict by-law, a breach of which was punishable by death. Women were especially protected, a certain place being set apart for their exclusive use, as a place was set apart at one side of the lists of medieval tournaments for the Queen of Beauty and the other ladies.

At the opening of the assembly there was always a solemn proclamation of peace, and the king who held the fair awarded prizes to the most successful poets, musicians, and professors and masters of every art.' — See Dr Sullivan's Introduction to O'Curry's *Lectures*.

12. *The Contest of the Bards.*

'The three musical feats of the *Daghda*, a celebrated de Danaan chief and Druid, were the *Suantraighe*, which from its deep murmuring caused sleep. The *Goltraighe*, which from its meltive plaintiveness caused weeping, and the Goltraighe, which from its merriment caused laughter.

Bose, the great Norse harper, could give on his harp the Gyarslager, or stroke of the sea gods, which produced mermaid's music.' — O'Curry's *Lectures*.

IRISH FAIRY STORIES
for Children

Edmund Leamy

In these stories we read all about the exciting adventures of Irish children in fairyland. We meet the fairy minstrel, giants, leprechauns, fairy queens and wonderful talking animals in Tir na nÓg.

IRISH FOLK STORIES
for Children

T. Crofton Croker

A selection of well-loved tales, including 'The Giant's Stairs', 'The Legend of Bottle-Hill', 'Rent Day' and 'Fíor Usga'.

The Children's Book of
IRISH FAIRY TALES

Patricia Dunn

The five exciting stories in this book tell of the mythical, enchanted origins of Irish landmarks when the countryside was peopled with good fairies, wicked witches, gallant heroes and beautiful princesses.

Mercier Press is the oldest independent Irish
publishing house and has published books in the
fields of history, literature, folklore, music, art,
humour, drama, politics, current affairs, law
and religion. It was founded in 1944 by John
and Mary Feehan.

In the building up of a country
few needs are as great as that of a publishing
house which would make the people proud of
their past, and proud of themselves as a people
capable of inspiring and supporting a world of
books which was their very own. Mercier Press
has tried to be that publishing house. On the
occasion of our fiftieth anniversary we thank
the many writers and readers who have
supported us and contributed to our success.

We face our second half-century
with confidence.